For John Baity (1937-2006)

# ACKNOWLEDGEMENTS

The alpha to this project is Dottie Caster, who reintroduced me to the fascinating game of bridge. The omega is Ray Lee, whose firm editorial hand caught more errors than I'd care to admit (any remaining are all on me). His insightful questions and comments sifted wheat from chaff and added seasoning when needed.

In between are all the people (too numerous to name, but you and I know who you are) who read (i.e. suffered through) early drafts, made suggestions for improvements and provided encouragement when I needed it.

And then there is Jan Rubens. In addition to everything it normally takes to put up with me, she provided unstinting patience and time to read and correct the manuscript 'one last time'. How did I get so lucky?

# TABLE OF CONTENTS

# INTRODUCTION

If you already earn many firsts at your club and in tournaments, congratulations — this book is probably not for you. However, if you are new to duplicate bridge, or don't earn **masterpoints**\* as often as you would like, or you are doing okay at the club but not in tournaments, this book will help you score better and have more fun along the way.

Some people are so gifted they breeze through the ranks and go on to challenge for national titles. Others study diligently and despite all their efforts discover bridge is not their game. This book is for the vast majority of us who fit between those two extremes. I am not one of the Grand Poobahs of bridge, nor will I ever be. I'm a regular guy, put my pants on one leg at a time, and I made a lot of mistakes along the way to becoming a **Life Master**. You'll read about some of them in this book. If we learn from our mistakes and (even better) from the mistakes of others, if we apply what we have learned when we sit down at the table, and if we find some compatible partners and teammates, we can become better bridge players.

I first played bridge in high school (1963-8). Four of us gathered on weekend nights or summer evenings at the kitchen table and played for hours. We used a simplified Goren bidding system. I have no idea how good (or more likely bad) our rubber bridge was, but we had a lot of fun. I did not play bridge in college, but in the mid-seventies one of my co-workers, Len Carusi, talked me into joining him to play duplicate a few times at a local New Jersey club. We thought we were pretty sophisticated: we used Stayman and Jacoby Transfers after our one notrump openings.

Flash forward to January 4, 2006. I had been playing backgammon online and was in the process of writing a novel. Consequently, I was spending a lot of solitary time and needed more social activity than backgammon provided. I wondered if bridge might be a good fit. Put a thought out there and the universe tends to respond. My Kentucky neighbor, Dottie Caster, asked me to fill in at a Wednesday social bridge game despite knowing I had not played a hand for almost thirty years. I wasn't first or last that day and had a thoroughly enjoyable time. One of the players offered to take me to the Northern Kentucky Bridge Club in Elsmere, KY to play duplicate, which she thought I would like. I remembered having fun with Len way back in the dark ages and said sure.

I joined the **ACBL** and quickly boned up on bidding, switching overnight from four-card majors and strong two-level openings to five-card majors and weak two-

---

\* Bridge is full of arcane terms, some of which you may not have encountered if you are new to duplicate bridge. The Glossary contains definitions for the words or phrases that are printed in bold type the first time they appear.

bids. People were friendly (a big change from the mid-seventies) and I was hooked. On January 17, 2006, I scored my first masterpoints when Gayle McCann dragged our partnership to a third place finish.

On October 23, 2007, I earned my 300th masterpoint and, having already fulfilled the other requirements, I became a Life Master. Along the way, I won some events and even scored a 75.86% game with Hank Greenwood at the Superiorland Bridge Club in Marquette, MI. Mostly, I earned my points with seconds and thirds and fourths.

No matter what a person's skill level is, bridge provides continual opportunities to learn. I'll be the first to admit (and my partners will heartily concur) that I still have much to learn about the game. Along the way to my gold card, however, I picked up a number of key points — tricks if you will — that helped me start winning more often at bridge. In this book, I will share those with you.

The book is divided into six sections: the first five cover bidding, declarer play, defense, strategy for pairs games and team games, and partnership issues. The last section, Try These, consists of practice deals. The examples are mostly from actual play and many of them are included because someone at the table made an error. Lots of the errors are mine, but many are by my partners. This is not because my partners routinely play poorly; they don't. However, I find it easier to spot errors in someone else's play and make a quick note than to figure out what I did wrong while I am making the plays! Believe me, all my partners could write books too...

Now let's get started.

# Chapter 1:

# SECRETS OF SUCCESSFUL BIDDING

Teachers I have spoken with say they give more lessons about bidding than anything else. That makes a lot of sense. Good coaching can certainly improve defense or declarer play, but bidding is like learning a new language and you have to use it on every deal you play, even if all you do is pass.

At the Harris, MI regional in 2007 I attended a workshop by Audrey Grant in which she presented a hand for the dealer with the following cards:

♠K9752 ♡Q6 ◇KQ964 ♣10

With these cards, would you open the bidding or pass?

She asked those who would open the bidding to raise their hands. About half the class did. She then asked who would pass, and the other half raised their hands. (For this discussion we will ignore the few unwilling to commit.) What was the right answer?

She said, 'Look around the room and choose your partners from those who raised their hands at the same time you did!'

## BIDDING BASIC #1:
### Play with someone who agrees with you on what a bid means.

The main purpose of partnership bidding is for partners to describe their hands and come to a conclusion about what contract they choose to play on that deal. In Chapter 5 we'll discuss a process for agreeing on a **convention card** with your partner, which is the first step.

Much of your partnership bidding understanding comes from your initial discussion of your partnership convention card, but not all of it. You would like to avoid a bidding disaster like this one I participated in soon after I started playing. I was sitting West:

| | West | North | East | South |
|---|---|---|---|---|
| | 1♠ | pass | 1NT[1] | pass |
| | 2◇ | all pass | | |

1. Forcing.

Making thirteen tricks, for 190 points and a stone cold bottom. Oops. I had 21 HCP (high card points) and I incorrectly thought the 2◇ bid was forcing. My partner thought I was giving her a choice of spades or diamonds and with five diamonds and few points, she passed. Oh well, at least it was a pairs game and my bad bid only affected our score on that one deal. We managed to take first in the event despite that 'oops'.

What would be a true catastrophe is if we had this same misunderstanding a second time. I made a quick note on my scoresheet to discuss the bidding after play was over, and while we waited for results we came to an agreement on what my bid would mean to both of us in the future (i.e. I asked for and received a bidding lesson!).

Our willingness to go back, face our disaster and discuss it, allowed us to avoid the same mistaken communication in the future. Gaining understanding of what you and your partner mean by every bid is a gradual, evolving process.

I mentioned that this deal came from a pairs game and so our score only affected that particular deal. There are a number of different scoring systems used in bridge. The kitchen bridge I played in high school used rubber bridge scoring, where results from previous deals are carried forward. In duplicate bridge, each deal is scored without regard to any previous results. In most pairs games the scores for each board are converted to **matchpoints** (MPs) to indicate how well your pair scored that deal compared to all other pairs holding the same cards. Team games convert scores to International Matchpoints (**IMPs**).

You can find more about how MPs and IMPs are calculated in Chapter 4. These different scoring schemes can affect both bidding and cardplay, and we'll discuss that in Chapter 4 as well. In this book, assume the deal is from a team game and the scoring is in IMPs, unless you are specifically told it's not. What that means is that as declarer, making your contract is critical, and you shouldn't worry about overtricks. Similarly, on defense you should do everything possible to defeat the contract.

## BIDDING BASIC #2:
### Fully bid your hand, but only once.

In the bidding disaster I described above, I committed one of the two major sins of bad bidding: I failed to let my partner know how strong my hand was. The 2◇ bid did not describe my extra values and my partner had no way of knowing I had a 21-point hand. It looked like fewer points to her, and she correctly passed.

Regardless of what bidding system you choose, make sure you understand how to show and recognize extra values through your bids. On an average day at the bridge table we don't get too many hands with 21 points; it's a shame to spoil them with bad bidding that doesn't describe to partner how strong we are.

The more common sin players commit is bidding the same values in their hand twice. We fall in love with our hand; we don't like what partner bid and want to rescue them from disaster; we hate to turn down any invitation to game. Whenever I hear the following bidding from an **I/N** (Intermediate/Novice) pair, my first inclination is to double.

| West | North | East | South |
|------|-------|------|-------|
| 1♠ | pass | 2♠ | pass |
| 3♠ | pass | 4♠ | all pass |

Often they are too high because one or the other partner has bid the same values twice. In all likelihood they should have stopped at 2♠ or 3♠. Of course, sometimes this is exactly the right bidding: both West and East hold hands at the tops of their ranges and they are lucky enough to have their high cards spread among the suits so North-South can't run off four quick tricks.

Here's an example of the kinds of hands that can get I/N players into trouble:

| ♠ K Q 9 6 4 3 | | ♠ A 10 7 5 |
|---------------|---|------------|
| ♡ Q 3 2 | N | ♡ 8 7 6 |
| ◊ A J 8 | W  E | ◊ K Q 4 |
| ♣ Q | S | ♣ 10 8 7 |

With six spades and opening points, West bids 1♠. East has 9 HCP with flat distribution — not enough for an invitational bid, but plenty to happily raise partner's suit — and so bids 2♠. Once East supports spades, West's hand becomes more valuable, but not strong enough to jump directly to 4♠. West would really love to know what his partner has in hearts but doesn't yet know any way to get that information. If West were to pass, he would be underbidding his hand. He doesn't have any other four-card suits but does have six spades, and so he invites to game by bidding 3♠.

So far, so good. East's job is to accept or reject his partner's invitation to game. If East is at the top of his range, he should accept. At the bottom he should reject. And here he is with 9 HCP, four-card trump support and a couple of tens. He convinces himself that those bounties outweigh the fact that with a flat hand about the only advantage his fourth trump has is that the opponents don't have it. He bids 4♠.

Following is the full deal. When the dust settles, East-West are down one because their combined ten trumps only took six tricks. East's flat hand did not allow any of his trumps to score as ruffs.

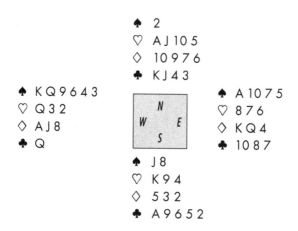

Overbidding one's hand can come in many forms. Let's look at this actual bidding example from a club pairs game with North-South vulnerable:

| West | North | East | South |
|------|-------|------|-------|
| | | 2♡¹ | pass |
| pass | dbl² | pass | pass³ |
| 3◇⁴ | dbl | 3♡⁴ | pass |
| pass | dbl | all pass | |

1. Weak bid showing six hearts and 5-10 HCP.
2. Asking partner to bid his best suit.
3. Preferring to play the doubled heart contract.
4. Decides to 'rescue' partner.

Here's the full deal:

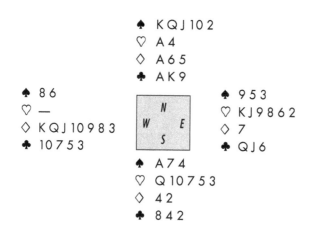

## Bidding analysis:

East has a decent preemptive 2♥ bid with 7 HCP, six hearts and **favorable vulnerability**. South has nothing to say and passes. Without support in hearts, West passes, remembering the admonition not to preempt a preempt. North has the power hand with 21 HCP and doubles with the intention of bidding spades later. South is looking at a hand of only 6 HCP, but with a five-card heart suit containing two honors. Without any four-card suit to bid, he decides to pass and defend the 2♥ doubled contract.

West counts HCP: West's 6 HCP added to East's 5-10 yields only 11-16, meaning North-South have 24-29 HCP. He correctly figures his diamonds will be worthless to his partner. He also looks at spades: he only has two, and his partner's heart preempt often means she has at most three. North-South appear to have at least an eight-card spade fit and can probably make a game in spades. West thinks the 2♥ doubled could go for -800 or -1100. In diamonds West has at least six winners. He bids 3♦, figuring if doubled it can go down no worse than three for a -500 score, better than either 2♥ doubled or the opponents making a vulnerable game in spades (at least -620). This is a well-considered bid.

North contemplates bidding his spades, but decides instead to double again and see what his partner does. East apparently does not trust her partner and makes a serious mistake. She rebids her hearts, violating the rule about not rebidding her values. She has told her partner everything about her hand with her first bid. She defined her heart suit length at six (it didn't get any longer); she defined her HCP at 5-10 (and they didn't get any stronger). She is not reevaluating her hand based on her partner's diamond bid, which might be a source of extra values. She ignored that her partner knew all about her hand, and still chose to bid diamonds rather than play in hearts. Despite her singleton diamond she 'rescued' her partner and rebid hearts.

South passed, letting North, with all the points, decide what to do. North figured if South was happy to play in 2♥ doubled, then 3♥ doubled is 200 points better and dropped another **red X** card on the table.

## Result:

East-West went down four tricks for -800 (with perfect defense North-South could actually have set their opponents by five tricks for -1100), a worse score than any possible game North-South could have bid. Incidentally, 3♦ probably goes down only one if South passes the double (which he shouldn't do).

Sometimes bidding mistakes happen because we fall in love with our hands. Here's one in which I was the guilty party. The opponents were vulnerable, and I sat North in third seat. Here was my hand:

♠ K 10 9 4 2   ♥ A K 10   ♦ A 5   ♣ Q 9 7

Both my partner and my right-hand opponent (**RHO**) passed. I opened with 1♠ (some partnerships would open 1NT, but our partnership agreement did not allow 1NT with a five-card major). My left-hand opponent (**LHO**) passed and my partner made a simple raise to 2♠. Under our very basic convention card her raise indicates **dummy points** ranging from 6 to a bad 10. I didn't have a second suit to bid; we didn't play any conventions to allow me to ask how strong her hand was. I hated to bid spades again, which would generally indicate six of them. I figured if she had 8 or more points we would have game. Heck, I only had 16 HCP (and 17 total points, giving myself 1 point for the extra length in spades), that left 24 HCP between the other three players, surely my partner would have her fair share. If she had 8 points, we could probably make game — and with that thought I bid 4♠.

Now, I've already confessed to falling in love with my hand. In order to justify bidding 4♠, I needed my bid to be correct if my partner had the minimum of her possible point range. If she had only 6 points could we make game? Not likely. So since I didn't have enough for a sure game, should I have passed 2♠?

No. My partner might have had enough points for game and my passing 2♠ wouldn't give her an opportunity to let me know her actual strength. I needed to make an invitational bid and let my partner decide whether to accept or not. Even if she had minimum values, we should be able to make nine tricks, so I wasn't putting us in a situation where we were liable to go down because I bid.

What should I have done? Any bid I made would have been something of a lie since I didn't have six spades or four of any other suit. Here's where it helps to apply Bidding Basic #1 and have partnership agreements. Depending on your partnership style you could try 3♣ or 3♠. Sometimes you don't know how your partner will take your bid, so you have to pick whichever option you think is most descriptive (and least confusing) to your partner. In situations like this, many experts say you are better off lying about your minor than your major and would suggest the 3♣ bid. (Of course, the experts would have bidding agreements to cover the situation.)

One of my all-time favorite agreements for new partnerships is the ASBAF (pronounced 'as-baff') convention. It stands for **All Strange Bids Are Forcing**. With a new partner, if I don't have a clue what a bid means, I assume it is forcing and bid again. With luck, her next bid will be clearer!

Here's the full deal.

```
                    ♠ K 10 9 4 2
                    ♡ A K 10
                    ◇ A 5
                    ♣ Q 9 7
   ♠ Q 7 5          ┌─────────┐      ♠ A 8
   ♡ 7 6 5 4        │    N    │      ♡ J 9 3 2
   ◇ Q J 4 2        │ W     E │      ◇ K 9 8 6
   ♣ A 4            │    S    │      ♣ J 8 3
                    └─────────┘
                    ♠ J 6 3
                    ♡ Q 8
                    ◇ 10 7 3
                    ♣ K 10 6 5 2
```

## Bidding analysis:

If you choose to bid 3♣ over 2♠, your partner might experience a rush of happy feelings since you bid her five-card suit. But once she thinks about it, she'll realize there are not enough combined partnership points for 5♣ or 3NT. From a scoring standpoint, 3♠ earns +140, whereas making 3♣ only scores +110. Since both contracts appear equally safe, your partner will correct the contract back to 3♠, at which point you'll pass. If you choose to bid 3♠ over 2♠, your partner passes.

Wait a minute, some of you may be saying right about now. You can make ten tricks on this deal if you make the right guesses in both spades and clubs. You are absolutely correct, and bidding and making 4♠ would be a wonderful score.

Bridge is a game of percentages. Good bridge is making the bids and plays that most often win. Justifying a bid based solely on its working in a particular example is bad bridge and is referred to as 'resulting'. Switch South's ♣10 for East's ♣8 on this deal, and you will have your work cut out to make nine tricks, let alone ten.

Sometimes you do luck out with a bad bid. Sometimes you bid perfectly and get an abysmal result. Most of the time bad bids produce bad results and good bids produce good results. Make sure when you are reviewing how you and your partner bid that you don't confuse correct bidding with lucky or unlucky results.

Let's look at another deal. With both sides vulnerable, you are sitting North holding:

♠ A J 8 4　♡ J 10 7 4　◇ A 9 3 2　♣ 5

Your LHO opens the auction with a pass. Partner opens 1♣. RHO passes and it's your call. Clubs was not the suit you wanted partner to suggest as trumps, but you do have 10 HCP and four cards in each of the other three suits. Some partnerships bid four-card suits up the line, but I have a preference to show majors when I have them. With four cards in both hearts and spades, I bid hearts first in response to partner's minor opening bid. It doesn't matter that the spades are a better suit — even if I had ♡5432, I'd still bid them first. So, 1♡ it is. Opponents continue to pass, and partner now bids 1♠.

| West | North | East | South |
|------|-------|------|-------|
| | | pass | 1♣ |
| pass | 1♡ | pass | 1♠ |
| pass | ? | | |

Before making your next bid, it is useful to consider what you have already learned about partner's hand. Partner's first bid indicated that she has an opening hand but not enough values for an artificial strong 2♣ opening. She has at least three clubs (since she opened them) and she doesn't have five of either major (unless she has six or more clubs). She did not open 1NT or 2NT so she doesn't have a balanced hand with either 15-17 HCP or 20-21 HCP.

Her second bid fills in more of the picture. She didn't support my hearts, which she would do if she had four of them. She showed four spades with her 1♠ bid and at the same time limited her hand to 12-17 points. Her hand is limited because of what she did not bid. Holding an unbalanced hand with 18+ points, she would have made a jump shift to 2♠. If she had a balanced hand with 18-19 HCP she would have chosen 2NT as her second bid to highlight her points rather than the four spades. Again, your partnership bidding agreements may differ a bit, but with a perfectly balanced 4-3-3-3 distribution and 12-14 points, partner might have chosen 1NT as her second bid.

So, we can conclude that partner has either a semi-balanced hand with 12-14 points or an unbalanced one with 12-17 points.

Now let's get back to your hand. Your first bid told partner you had at least 6 points and four or more hearts. With your second bid you must provide her additional information about your hand. You like spades and need to let her know that, and there's no reason to delay supporting spades.

Your HCP remain at 10. Does that mean you should bid 2♠ and hope maybe partner has enough to invite you to game, in which case you can happily accept?

Before you determine your second bid, you must reevaluate your hand. On your first bid you counted only HCP since you didn't have a fit with partner's clubs. Now, you must reevaluate your hand to reflect that you have a spade fit. You still have 10 HCP, but the singleton club now becomes an asset instead of a liability. You can add 2 dummy points for your singleton club. That gives you 12 dummy points.

If you only bid 2♠, you have understated the value of your hand. Partner will recognize that you too have four spades, but will assume you have no more than 9 (or a bad 10) dummy points. You will have hidden from her the value your singleton club brings to the partnership.

If you bid 2♠ and your partner has a hand like

♠KQ53  ♡Q82  ◇K10  ♣A1073

she will do the partnership addition. Her 14 points and your reported maximum do not add up to game values. She knows your side should be in a partscore and will pass. A bid of 2♠ violates Bidding Basic #2 because you have not fully bid your hand. You haven't provided partner accurate information with which to evaluate the partnership's total resources on the deal. When you look at your hands together — as a reminder, you held

♠AJ84  ♡J1074  ◇A932  ♣5

— you can see that ten tricks should come fairly easily unless there is a wicked trump split against you.

So if bidding 2♠ is too meek, what about jumping straight to game? Given your revised evaluation of 12 dummy points and what you know about partner's hand, can you be sure your side should be bidding game?

Nope. If partner has the low end of her range and a flattish hand, you'll need really good breaks (or very cooperative opponents) to make ten tricks in spades. Partner could easily have something like

♠KQ53  ♡862  ◇104  ♣AK73

Bidding 4♠ would be a serious overbid on your hand and would violate the principle of bidding your full values, but not more.

You don't have enough information from partner to know whether you should play this deal in a partial or game contract. Therefore, your responsibility with your next bid is to try to provide partner with enough information so she can make the decision.

With your revised dummy points now totaling 12, bidding 3♠ does a good job of describing your hand's value to partner. It shows you have four spades and 10-12 dummy points. Depending on what her hand looks like, she can pass or bid 4♠.

Partnerships (following Bidding Basic #1) should develop agreements about who should stretch for a bid and who needs to be more conservative. For example, one expert pair I know have the agreement that the inviter (the 3♠ bidder in our last example) is allowed to stretch just a bit if they think it appropriate. The partner who decides the final contract should not stretch. With this agreement, the partnership doesn't find itself in a situation where both hands have stretched and they reach too high; nor does it find itself missing makeable games because neither hand stretched a bit.

Some hands are easier to bid than others, as this next deal illustrates. West dealt and neither side is vulnerable. Sitting North with

♠ 10 7 2   ♡ K 10 3   ◇ Q 9 3   ♣ A Q 7 2

you hear your partner open 2♣ in fourth seat.

Let's say the system you are playing uses 2◇ as a waiting response, and that is what you bid. The opponents pass again and partner bids 3◇. Now before we proceed, what do you know about partner's hand? Once you determine that answer, what are you going to bid?

South's two bids told you a lot about her hand, but not everything you would like to know. Under many systems after a 2◇ waiting bid, opener will bid 2NT with a balanced 22-24 HCP and 3NT with a balanced 25-27 HCP. South's choice of 3◇ suggests an unbalanced hand with diamonds as her best suit. She has not limited her hand. She could even have a balanced hand with 28+ HCP.

Or she could have much less. Many pairs open 2♣ with eight and a half to nine playing tricks. I happen to like Marty Bergen's rule for opening 2♣ when you plan to bid a suit rather than notrump on your second round. His guideline is to bid 2♣ if you have at least four quick tricks (aces or ace-king combinations) and no more than four losers (where losers are missing aces, kings or queens up to the suit length). A hand such as

♠ A   ♡ A 8   ◇ A K J 10 6 4 2   ♣ K 10 3

would qualify under either definition even though it does not have 22 HCP.

Back to the current example, your partner could have a full 22+ point 2♣ opener that looks something like

♠ A K   ♡ A Q   ◇ A K J 10 6 4   ♣ K J 3

Because of the doubleton in both majors, perhaps she preferred to highlight diamonds rather than points.

So you know a lot, but there is much you don't know about partner's hand. What are you bidding?

Gosh, you have three-card diamond support with an honor; maybe you should show your support and bid 4◇. Of course you do have a flat hand and bidding 4◇ rules out playing in 3NT. You could bid 3NT. Surely it's better to need only nine tricks for game, rather than the two additional tricks required to make 5◇ — although your spades are a little weak.

Those are interesting questions, but I think they might be barking up the wrong tree. How many points do you have? How many points does partner know you have? Your hand has 11 HCP with flat distribution, so maybe it's not really worth 11 points — call it 10+. So far your partner doesn't know about any of them.

How many points does partner have? As discussed above, we don't know, but her bidding hasn't limited her point count. How likely is it that your points and partner's points total at least 33, enough for a small slam? There's a really good chance, so you shouldn't take an action that closes the auction, which bidding 3NT is likely to do. When this deal was actually played, three pairs did stop at 3NT.

I hope you decided to bid something to help your partner know you have a hand with some values and that you are considering slam. Let's agree you're not going to bid hearts or spades. That leaves either supporting the diamonds or bidding clubs. If you bid 4◇, maybe your partner will bid 4NT and you can tell her about your ♣A, which may allow her to bid 6◇. Of course, bidding 4◇ might only elicit a 5◇ response from partner, and then where are you?

You could bid 4♣. You have 6 HCP in clubs (nice), but you only have four clubs (naughty), and what are you going to do if your partner responds by bidding 4◇? Well heck, maybe you should bite the bullet and bid 4NT yourself and find out if your partner has the three missing aces. But if you take that approach, opposite an unlimited partner, you won't have enough information to know where to place the contract, so taking charge is probably not correct.

I didn't say this game was easy. If it were, who would want to play it? Pick your poison, but don't shut down the bidding before you let your partner know you are interested in exploring slam and don't presume to take command until partner has limited her hand.

This deal came from a pairs game and four pairs actually stopped in three of a minor! (My bet is those four Souths opened the bidding with 1◇ and then at least one person of the North-South pair didn't bid all of their values, violating Bidding Basic #2.)

Okay, before we look at all four hands, let's go back and follow what might happen if South opened 1◇. You have a pretty standard 2NT response. You hope your partner has enough points to bid 3NT, but instead she comes back and bids 4♣ (showing clubs and lots of points, not asking for aces!). Now what are you going to do?

Do you support your partner's clubs? Do you bid diamonds because they were your partner's first bid suit and are probably longer than her clubs? Given this bidding sequence, should you try for slam with the double fit? Double fits are nice and you have 8 HCP in partner's suits, but if South has five diamonds and four clubs, she still has four cards in the majors — and in the majors you have losers galore.

At the time I played the deal, had my partner opened 1◇ and then bid 4♣, I would have made the mistake of thinking I had to solve the problem of placing the contract and bid 5◇. That decision violates Bidding Basic #2 by withholding the true value of my hand from partner. A 5◇ bid unilaterally closes the auction, eliminating the chance for partner to reevaluate her hand after I tell her more about my hand. A 4◇ bid would be better, and given South's hand, will be sufficient to elicit a 4NT bid and an eventual slam contract.

In the actual play, five pairs ended up in game and the remaining five pairs reached small slam contracts: two in clubs and three in notrump.

Here are all four hands:

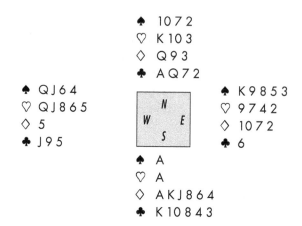

As you can see, North-South can make 7♣, 7◇ or 7NT regardless of the opening lead. Consequently, those who bid 6NT scored better than those in 6♣ and 6◇. Despite that outcome, I think 6NT was a risky contract to bid (well, before seeing all four hands) and would have preferred to bid 6♣ or 6◇. Suit slams are often easier to make than those in notrump because you can use your trump superiority to set up a long suit or avoid losers in a short suit.

Rearranging a few cards without changing point counts in any hand, we might have the four hands looking like this:

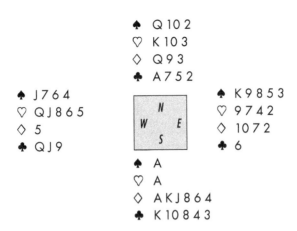

```
              ♠ Q 10 2
              ♡ K 10 3
              ◇ Q 9 3
              ♣ A 7 5 2

♠ J 7 6 4          N          ♠ K 9 8 5 3
♡ Q J 8 6 5    W       E      ♡ 9 7 4 2
◇ 5                S          ◇ 10 7 2
♣ Q J 9                       ♣ 6

              ♠ A
              ♡ A
              ◇ A K J 8 6 4
              ♣ K 10 8 4 3
```

South's hand has not changed. North has exactly the same distribution, but traded the ♣Q to West for the ♠Q. Poof: 6♣ and 6◇ still make, but North-South can only make eleven tricks in notrump on a spade lead.

In general, when you bid slams, bid the safest slam. Sure, this time 6NT works and garners a tie for top, but bidding a small slam in either minor suit scores nearly as well. Keep in mind that in actual play, twelve pairs didn't bid any slam! If the cards had been as in the revised deal, your minor-suit slam makes and 6NT can go down. Bidding the safe slam is good odds.

As an aside, many experts holding South's cards would choose to open the bidding 1◇ rather than 2♣. Very strong hands featuring either a minor suit or two suits are notoriously difficult to bid after a 2♣ opening followed by whatever conventional response partner makes. Jeez, but what if your 1◇ bid is passed out? You could miss a game. The chances of being passed out are very slim. You have only two of the twenty-six cards in the majors — someone at the table will bid a major, and you will have a second bid to show your strength.

When you first start out, most of the bidding errors will be yours. Asking questions about your current bidding is one way to learn to bid better. A second way is to add more conventions to your arsenal.

When I returned to bridge after my thirty-plus-year layoff, I had to throw out most of the bidding I knew and adopt more modern bidding techniques. I quickly learned a serviceable set of conventions that I could play. But opponents were doing things that made my life difficult. I would open 1♣, my LHO would bid 2♣, my partner might or might not bid something and before I knew it the opponents were bidding and making 4♡ with fewer than half the points in the deck.

They knew something I didn't know, something I was going to have to learn if I wanted to get better. If you want to improve, you too may have to learn more conventions. I have heard many I/N players in the clubs and at tournaments make excuses for not learning new conventions. They are all bunk.

Each convention you add has advantages and disadvantages. The primary advantage of a new convention is to allow you to describe some aspect of your hand in a more thorough or efficient manner. The probable price of adding a new convention is that you eliminate a natural bid, and if you are like me, while you learn the convention, you'll make a number of mistakes you hadn't made before. And if you add too many conventions, you run the risk of confusion or lapses of memory.

While you are learning a new convention, keep in mind:

## BIDDING BASIC #3:
### Learning a new bidding convention is a four-step process.

### Step 1: Learn the *entire* convention.
Whether you study the convention by reading a book, using online materials, or learn by taking a class or through informal discussions with a fellow player, the key is to learn the *entire* convention. Early on, I 'learned' the **Jacoby 2NT** convention to respond to a one-level major suit opening bid by partner. This allows you to show at least four-card support for the major and sufficient points to suggest the partnership should be in game. It also takes up bidding room from the opponents. How useful, I thought, and immediately entered it onto my convention card.

Only several months later while discussing my card with a new partner did she ask me if I knew what to respond if she made a Jacoby 2NT bid.

I had no clue.

Another lesson learned. Now if I want to explore a new convention I set up a bunch of 3x5 cards with the various response permutations and combinations and I go through the cards until I am getting them right. Then I move to Step 2.

### Step 2: We've put it on the convention card, but in reality, I'm still not quite ready.
For me, the next step is to commit to playing the convention and agreeing with a partner to have it on our card. Unfortunately, adding the convention to my card does not automatically mean I remember to apply it correctly. I miss it when I should use it. I miss it when my partner bids it. I get a terrible result on a deal (or occasionally luck out), but the pain of the debacle helps reinforce the convention and soon I move to Step 3.

### Step 3: Recognize when partner uses the convention.
One day it happens. Partner makes the conventional bid. I remember to **alert** it (assuming it is alertable) and a short burst of energy courses through my system as I realize I have made a small bit of progress. Finally I move to Step 4.

### Step 4: I use the convention when I should.

Sometimes a Step 3.5 intrudes: I use the convention when I should but also use it occasionally when I should not. That step is short, punctuated by an abysmal score or two with the resulting scars. Finally, I have the convention learned.

Almost.

Some conventions I use infrequently because most of my partners play something different, or it does not come up often. For example, in my part of Michigan, most players use a 2NT response to partner's weak two-bid to ask for a 'feature' — a side honor that might fit responder's hand. In Northern Kentucky they play the 2NT response as Ogust, a method that asks about hand strength and suit quality. Whenever I am returning to play with my Kentucky friends, I make a special effort to review Ogust before sitting down at the table.

Maybe you are better than I am and can move directly from Step 1 to Step 4. I haven't yet, although I have shortened the time I spend in Step 2 and Step 3 purgatory. Now when I introduce something new, I don't get upset if I miss a bid. I recognize I am making progress toward Step 4. I dust myself off and remind myself I am that much closer to mastering the darned thing and pick up the next hand.

### BIDDING BASIC #4:
## Methodically add conventions.

Periodically add new conventions to your knowledge base. Seek out players who play the convention you want to learn and play with them.

Sometimes the reason to learn a convention is so that you understand what opponents are doing a little better, even though you have no expectation of playing it yourself. We have a couple of players at both the Michigan and Kentucky clubs who play the Precision bidding system — not my cup of tea and at my current level not worth the effort to memorize all the bids available. By gaining some familiarity with their system, however, I understand their bidding better and can learn how to compete in their auctions in productive ways.

Do not add conventions willy-nilly. Most conventions require trading off a natural bid for the additional information provided by the conventional bid. A simple example of this is the Stayman convention after a 1NT opener by partner. By using the Stayman 2♣, your partnership eliminates the possibility of playing a 2♣ contract after a 1NT opener. Sometimes 2♣ is the only contract that makes for your side but putting Stayman on your convention card eliminates this.

How often is 2♣ the only makeable contract after partner opens 1NT? Very, very infrequently, which is why most partnerships are happy to abandon a natural 2♣ bid after partner's 1NT opener and exchange it for the Stayman 2♣ major-fit seeking bid.

Ask the advice of a teacher or some of the stronger players at your club about what you should learn next and why. The 'why?' portion of your information gathering is important. If you understand the rationale for using a particular convention, you will learn it much more quickly and easily. After asking for and considering the advice, decide what you want to learn and go about doing it.

Here's a quote from Larry Cohen to keep in mind:

*If you're a 19-year old physics major at M.I.T with a photographic memory, and you have a comparable partner, then by all means fill out the most complicated system card that you dare to. If you're anyone else, do yourself a favor and stick to the basics. KISS. (KISS = keep it simple, Stupid.)*

At one point I tried to add several conventions at the same time. I had done my flashcard preparation and was all set... until I sat down at the table. Faced with having to remember all the new possible bids, I messed up big-time and compounded my mistakes by taking myself to task for forgetting. Nothing like a little self-flagellation to destroy any chance of improving.

Another lesson learned: *add new conventions slowly.* Stop and lock one new understanding in place before you add the next piece. Like in *Aesop's Fables*, the tortoise with a slow and steady pace will beat the hare.

When you play a convention with a new partner, it's important to make sure you're both on the same page when it comes to auctions involving conventional bids. I already mentioned my lack of knowledge about the continuations after a Jacoby 2NT response. I also want to make sure my partner and I have the same understandings about what all the bids mean. Jacoby 2NT is a good example of a convention that people play with many little variations. Make sure you and partner have agreed on all aspects of a convention before you add it to your card.

I recently had a misunderstanding crop up after a fourth-suit game force bid. My partner was a more experienced player and I assumed (not making an *ass* out of *you*, but potentially making one out of *me*) that we agreed on the preferred structure after the fourth-suit forcing bid. After the deal was over, we both made a note to discuss the next bids since we clearly didn't agree. I was lucky that time because we stumbled into the correct game contract, but I am convinced the path to rotten scores is paved with 'good' assumptions. After you play a new convention for a while, you may come to understand additional nuances and develop further issues to discuss with partner. But hey, that's one of the pleasures of learning — it's a continual process.

## BIDDING BASIC #5:
### Learn to compete.

Parents teach us it is impolite to interrupt a conversation and some I/N pairs seem to think this applies when their opponents start the bidding. If their RHO opens, it would be rude (they think) to bid themselves because it would interfere with their opponents having a nice conversation to determine what contract they should be in.

I hope you know I've tucked my tongue firmly into my cheek when I say it would be rude. It is perfectly acceptable, even laudatory, to interrupt your opponents while they bid. You do it by making bids of your own.

Here are three advantages:

1) Sometimes you and your partner have a good fit in a suit or even a majority of the points and should be the ones playing the deal. If you never bid after your opponents open, you'll never find out — that would be a bad thing.
2) Your bidding may make it more difficult for the opponents to find their best contract — that would be a good thing.
3) Your bids may help your partner find the perfect lead to set the opponents' contract.

Often I/Ns say something like, 'But my opponent has opening points. Unless I have opening points too, how can I compete? They might set me.'

Maybe they will, but going down one or two tricks if your opponents belonged in game may give you a great result.

Let's look at some examples. Your RHO opens 1♣. On each hand, what would you bid* and why?

| | |
|---|---|
| 1. | ♠KQ1043 ♡1094 ◇A62 ♣98 |
| 2. | ♠K1043 ♡Q94 ◇A62 ♣984 |
| 3. | ♠AK43 ♡Q1094 ◇A62 ♣98 |
| 4. | ♠KQ104032 ♡1094 ◇J62 ♣9 |
| 5. | ♠KQ10432 ♡AK4 ◇J6 ♣98 |
| 6. | ♠KQ104 ♡Q104 ◇AQ62 ♣98 |
| 7. | ♠K104 ♡Q94 ◇AQ1062 ♣98 |
| 8. | ♠K104 ♡A94 ◇98 ♣AQ1062 |
| 9. | ♠87653 ♡K94 ◇K62 ♣98 |
| 10. | ♠8765 ♡8765 ◇AKJ ♣AQ |

1. Bid 1♠. You have 9 HCP and a decent five-card spade suit. Whatcha waitin' for? As part of your partnership agreement you need to determine the minimum number of points necessary to make an overcall. I have partners who require 8 HCP. Others (and this would be my personal preference) are comfortable with 6 as long as you're not embarrassed by the suit and the vulnerability is right. With enough experience you and your partner (remembering Bidding Basic #1 about playing with partners who agree with you on what a bid means) will decide your combined comfort level.

---

* Technically, I'm asking for your 'call'. A 'bid' only includes 1♣ through 7NT and does not include pass, double or redouble. Throughout the book we'll ignore the strict interpretation and refer to all calls as bids.

Make sure you aren't like some folks I've met who wouldn't overcall on this hand because it doesn't have opening points. This hand is much too strong to pass.

2. Pass. This has the same 9 HCP but no five-card suit. If partner bids one of the other three suits, you may show support later, but for now your best action is to pass and see what transpires.

3. Double. With 13 HCP, four cards in each major and three diamonds, it doesn't get much better than this for a fine takeout double. You have good support for whatever suit your partner bids.

4. Bid 2♠. With six spades and 6 HCP, you would have made a weak two opening if you had been the first bidder with this hand. Why should you make a weak two-bid? To preempt your opponents and make it harder for them to find their best contract. In first seat when you bid 2♠, you don't know if you are preempting the opponents or your partner since no one else has bid. In first seat, the chances are 2-1 in your favor that you are preempting your opponents rather than your partner. When your RHO opens the bidding, the betting line becomes even stronger that the opponents have the majority of the points.

If you don't barge your way into their conversation and bid 2♠, your opponents have a full selection of bids to describe their hands. Instead, picture yourself stepping between them and extending your elbows to keep them apart. Your 2♠ bid eliminates 1◇, 1♡, 1♠, 1NT, 2♣, 2◇, 2♡ and 2♠ from responder's choices. (Although you hope they weren't planning on bidding spades!) The price is small. You've given them two calls they didn't previously have: they can double your 2♠ bid or cuebid 3♠. I like those odds, so spread your elbows to their full width with these cards and bid 2♠.

5. Bid 1♠. The addition of the ♡AK compared to hand #4 makes this hand way too strong to preempt. Remember Bidding Basic #2 — fully bid your hand. If you preempt, you are understating the value of your hand. Your hand is strong enough with 13 HCP and six spades to rebid spades at the two-level when the bidding comes around to you again. When you bid 1♠, your partner will not know whether your hand looks like #1 or #5 — your overcall has a wide range. With hand #1, you can bid once (unless your partner makes a forcing bid). With hand #5 and its extra values, you may be able to bid again.

6. Double. Not as good a shape for a takeout double as hand #3 because you have only three hearts; but with 13 HCP, only two clubs and support for whatever your partner bids, you need to enter the auction. With an opening hand you should bid if you possibly can.

7. Bid 1◇. You wish you had the majors, but diamonds are what you have. Your elbows are tucked in pretty close to your body with this bid, but even if your side doesn't win the auction, you would be very happy if your partner led diamonds when she had the chance.

8. Pass. You have an opening hand, but since RHO stole your bid, you are out of luck. Remember, a double here would be for takeout, and you're not strong enough for a 1NT overcall. Who knows at this point how the bidding will turn out, but for now you need to sit on your hands and pass smoothly.

9. Pass. What, didn't I say I like to overcall on 6 HCP? Yep, but I also specified that I wanted to have a halfway decent suit. Five spades to the eight do not qualify in my book as a decent suit.

10. Double. Yes, I know the four-card majors are weaker than the kid at the beach the bullies kicked sand at. Doesn't matter. This hand has 14 HCP including the ♣AQ **tenace** sitting behind the club opener. My partner might have a five-card major, in which case we have at least a nine-card fit. Even if she ends up bidding diamonds with only four, I have three nice ones. Call me optimistic, but I'm hoping we get to play this one, not the opponents.

With those examples under your belt, I hope you'll feel a bit more confident about entering the auction when your RHO bids. Now let's look at another situation that comes up a lot. Early in my playing career, sitting in second seat, I would pick up a hand like

♠K982  ♡106  ◇AJ96  ♣Q109

with both sides not vulnerable.

My RHO opens 1♡. With too little for a takeout double and no five-card suit, I pass. LHO raises to 2♡. That gets passed around to me and I pass again. The opponents take eight or nine tricks and we end up with a poor score. I'd scratch my head and try to figure out where our defense allowed them to take an extra trick. But the problem wasn't our defense; the problem was my bidding.

| West | North | East | South |
|------|-------|------|-------|
|      |       | 1♡   | pass  |
| 2♡   | pass  | pass | ?     |

Given the bidding, my RHO had a minimum opener and my LHO had heart support and fewer than 10 points. Combined, they probably have 18-24 points.

On average they have 20-22 points between them; my partner and I have 18-20 points. Why should we let them play this hand in 2♡?

Let's say our opponents can make 3♡ 75% of the time and only 2♡ 25% of the time. If I don't bid, 75% of the time we score -140 and the rest of the time we score -110. Now, what happens if I reopen the bidding with a double and force my partner to bid? (Unless of course she is sitting on a heart stack, in which case she'll pass.) She will have four of some suit and often five; generally we'll have at least an eight-card fit, although occasionally we'll end up with a seven-card trump suit. Let's assume the worst and she bids 3♣ on 3-3-3-4 distribution.

Any time you decide to reopen the bidding, as I suggest you should do in this example, there is always a trade-off between the potential rewards and the risks. So what can happen after we stick our nose in their auction? Often the opponents will bid on to 3♡ and still win the contract. Three-quarters of the time they'll make their bid and score the same as if we had not reopened the bidding: -140 for us. But 25% of the time we set them: +50 for us — a clear gain because of the reopening double.

Before we explore this example further, I should note that we'll talk more about these reopening bids in Chapter 4. At that point we'll discuss how the different scoring methods affect our decision to reopen. For now, let's just look at whether or not bidding improves our score. What if they leave us in 3♣? Here are several of the most likely results:

We make 3♣ for a score of +110 (a whole lot better than -110 or -140).
We go down one for a score of -50 (much better than -110 or -140).
We go down two for a score of -100 (a little better than -110 or -140).
We go down three for a score of -150 (not a good result).

If they double our 3♣ bid (fairly unlikely, but it does happen) here are the possible results:

We make 3♣ doubled for a score of +470 (three cheers for our side!).
We go down one for a score of -100 (a little better than -110 or -140).
We go down two for a score of -300 (ugly result, but we did it with class).

As with anything else I tried, I earned a few bad results before I developed enough experience to know when to let the opponents go on their merry way and when to compete. Even now, competing occasionally garners me a rotten result and is an area in which I still have a lot to learn. I consider those occasional poor results a small price to pay because, starting with the first game in which I became more aggressive in competitive bidding situations, my results improved — dramatically.

An added bonus of competing is you end up playing more hands — the favorite part of the game for many bridge players.

There are many forms of competing in addition to reopening the bidding. One of the most effective ways to get in the opponents' way is by preempting. Newer players often tell teachers that they don't like to preempt because they don't want to go down. As a result, they are often reluctant to preempt by bidding hands with long suits (six or more cards) and less than opening points.

Let's say with neither side vulnerable you are dealer as West with:

♠ A K J 7 6 4   ♡ 8 7 3   ♢ 10 9 4   ♣ 8

Any way you count the hand, you can't come close to an opening one-level bid. Perhaps you can sympathize with Timid Timothy, who feels it is too scary to preempt 2♠ with this hand. You could end up losing three hearts, three diamonds, and a club for seven tricks. Then, pessimist that you are, the ♠Q will be offside so your finesse will fail; partner will only have one spade (if that) and the opponents' spades will break 5-1. Gosh — maybe *they* can make 2♠. And worst of all, Timid Timothy is certain that any time he preempts he will surely be doubled.

So Timid passes and awaits the action. Maybe he'll be lucky and the bidding will go:

| West | North | East | South |
|------|-------|------|-------|
| pass | pass | pass | 1♡ |
| ? | | | |

Then Mr. Timothy with his six spades containing 8 HCP can comfortably overcall 1♠. That's what he was hoping for, right?

But it's quite possible the bidding could go:

| West | North | East | South |
|------|-------|------|-------|
| pass | 1♡ | pass | 3♡[1] |
| ? | | | |

1. Limit raise.

Now where's Timid's spade bid? Just a distant dream. No way can he enter the bidding at the three-level. Worse, Timid's partner East doesn't know Timid has potential spade tricks and must make her lead without that valuable knowledge.

If instead, Timid takes a deep breath (mentally, not physically, we don't want to be giving anything away at the table) and opens 2♠, let's see what happens.

North-South suddenly have a lot of pressure on them. Does North, in the direct overcall seat, have enough to bid at the three-level or make a takeout double? If not, does South have the points and the right shape to bid or reopen? Does East have a hand that is insufficient to overcall a 1♡ opener by North, but might justify a bid after West opens 2♠ because if spades are trumps her hand is worth more?

Without looking at everyone's cards, we don't know the specific answers to those questions, but we know for sure that neither North nor South can bid 1♡ — or even 2♡. The preemptive 2♠ bid has done its work.

What if everything that Timid Timothy worried about came true? He would take five tricks for down three and a -150 score. If his result is that bad, I'll bet most of the time the opponents missed bidding a game that would have scored them +400 or +420. Timid's 2♠ preempt kept them out of the game.

But wait, couldn't North-South just double Timid?

Yes, but it is fairly unlikely. Why? For all modern players, a double of an opening weak two-bid is for takeout, not penalty. For the double to stick, one of the opponents must have a hand that can make a takeout double over 2♠ and the other opponent must have a hand such that he ignores his partner's request to bid one of the three other suits and instead prefers to convert the takeout double into a penalty double. That combination is not impossible, but unlikely. The risk is small and the reward is large.

In this next deal, both pairs are vulnerable, Timothy (no longer Timid) decides to give this preemptive thing a try and, discovering he has exactly the same hand

♠ A K J 7 6 4　♡ 8 7 3　◇ 1 0 9 4　♣ 8

opens by bidding 2♠. North passes and you (as Timothy's partner) look at your sad collection:

♠ 1 0 9 5 3　♡ K　◇ 7 6　♣ Q J 9 7 6 4

| West | North | East | South |
|------|-------|------|-------|
| 2♠ | pass | ? | |

Is your first reaction 'oh, yuck'? With 6 HCP, composed of a singleton ♡K and a six-bagger club suit headed by the QJ, your 'yuck' response suggests you think you should pass as quickly as appears seemly.

My first reaction is to bid 4♠. Let me explain why. How many tricks will you take with your hand on defense? If you are lucky, North-South will finesse hearts and allow your singleton king to win the first heart trick. Maybe if you are really lucky you might score a club. Your spades and diamonds are worthless; maybe partner has something there.

How many spade tricks will your side score? At most one. Partner's 2♠ bid showed six spades; you have four, leaving them only three. The most favorable split is 2-1, so *if* partner has the ♠A (my partners always seem to think I should have that card), your side can take at most one spade trick. If spades are 3-0 or one of the opponents has the ♠A, you get no spade tricks.

Okay, so you don't have many defensive tricks, but maybe they won't be able to find a fit. Perhaps so, but since (formerly Timid) Timothy usually won't preempt in first seat with four of the other major, we can assume he has at most three hearts. You have one. That means North-South have at least nine. If they manage to bid at all, they are going to find that fit.

You have 6 HCP. Timid Timothy plays that a weak two-bid shows 5-10 HCP, so your side has somewhere between 11 and 16 HCP. That means they have 24-29 HCP and a nine-card heart fit, and one of them has a singleton or void in spades. That sounds like they have a very good chance for a heart game. Gosh, they might even have a slam.

If you follow my suggestion and raise Timothy to 4♠, then South has a problem even if he has lots of points. Entering the auction requires him to bid at the five-level. Furthermore, he doesn't know where the rest of the points are, because he doesn't know whether you bid 4♠ to further the preempt or whether you bid it expecting to make it because you have a strong hand.

That's the best you can do with your cards: cause South as much aggravation as possible.

Now, here's a fun activity you can try some rainy afternoon or evening. Take a deck of cards and display the East and West hands as shown. Take the remaining cards, shuffle and deal them out to North and South. Take the stronger of the two hands and give it to South. Then ask yourself, if you were South, would you be able to make a call after the 4♠ bid?

Below is a deal I came up with when I randomly distributed the North-South cards:

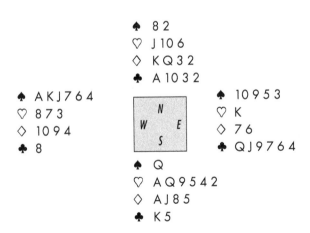

As you can see, North-South can make a small slam in hearts or diamonds, losing only the ♠A. In this particular deal, with 10 HCP and only three hearts, most Norths would not make a takeout double after West's 2♠ bid. After East bids 4♠, South is looking at 14 HCP (excluding the dead ♠Q) and a six-card heart suit.

South is slowly roasting on a pit of hot coals lit by your partner's 2♠ bid and made hotter by your 4♠ bid. Coming in at the five-level in hearts is a scary proposition. Although South knows it is a distributional deal, he has no clue who has the balance of the points, which means doubling is also a risky proposition. If West had passed or East had not extended the preempt to 4♠, South would have an easy heart bid and North-South would surely bid game, even if they didn't get to slam.

What can East-West make in spades? They will take eight or nine tricks, for -50 or -100 versus the sure -480 (or worse) if North-South are allowed to play in hearts.

So, if you are something of a Timid Timothy, try loosening up a bit and preempting more than you have in the past. I think you'll find your results improve. Do keep vulnerability in mind, though. Particularly if you are vulnerable and they are not, your preempt needs to be sound enough to avoid getting doubled.

Now that I have you all pumped up to compete in the bidding, I need to remind you to keep in mind Bidding Basic #2: *Fully bid your hand, but only once.*

On the next deal with East-West vulnerable, as South, you pick up an interesting collection:

♠9 ♡10 6 ◇A J 9 6 5 ♣Q 10 9 4 3

| West | North | East | South |
|------|-------|------|-------|
|      |       | 1♡   | 2NT[1] |
| 3♡   | 3♠    | dbl  | ?     |

1. Unusual 2NT showing at least 5-5 in the two lowest unbid suits, in this case the minors.

What do you bid?

Your partner understood your bid. The opponents have hearts and you have the minors, yet she still bid spades. What gives? Lots of possibilities, but I've learned in these situations the one thing I should not do is try to rescue my partner.

## BIDDING BASIC #6:

### If you have a misfit, pass.

You have no obligation to bid now that East has doubled. You should not bid 4♣, again giving a choice between clubs and diamonds. You should not bid 4◇ just because it is your stronger suit. For better or worse, partner has already rejected both of your suits.

You should not redouble 'for rescue', assuming that's the way partner would understand a redouble here.

You should pass and see what happens.

Maybe the opponents have 4♡ cold for -620 and 3♠ doubled goes down only three for -500. Maybe West will pull the double to 4♡ and you can set that one for +100. Maybe, maybe, maybe.

I repeat: you should pass and see what happens. Except in the rare situation where you should be in game, once you know there is a misfit, get out at the lowest level you can and hope it's not too high.

Sometimes, of course, even with a misfit you and your partner are so loaded with points that you should be playing in game. If sufficient transportation exists you might succeed in notrump, or maybe one of the suits is strong enough to stand on its own. In those cases, you can keep bidding, but when you are counting points in your hand and partner's suit will be trumps, count only high card points, not extra length. Your long suit may have no value at all.

Incorporate these six Bidding Basics into your game and watch your scores improve.

# Chapter 2:

# DARNED GOOD DECLARER PLAY

Congratulations, I think. You were the last one standing in the bidding contest and now you need to secure your contract, preferably with as many overtricks as you can. Or maybe you were sacrificing and you need to lose as few tricks as possible. Now what? The nine Declarer Devices in this chapter will help you gather all the tricks you deserve (and maybe even a few you don't deserve.)

## DECLARER DEVICE #1:
### Plan first, play second.

I'm sure you've heard or read that you must 'plan your play'. What exactly does that mean? It means stopping *before* you play to Trick 1 (really important!) and deciding on your basic approach to the play.

Here's what works for me in a suit contract.

1) Count losers, usually from the perspective of declarer's hand.
2) Assuming there are losers — how many times have you had thirteen tricks off the top? — try to figure out how to tuck them onto winning tricks in dummy.
3) Count entries between dummy and declarer to make sure there is sufficient transportation to get back and forth as many times as needed to carry out step (2).

In a notrump contract:

1) Start by counting immediate winners, which are usually far fewer than the contract requires.
2) Figure out likely places to develop more winners (generally through longer suits).
3) Make sure to figure out the entries in each hand needed to carry out your designed plan to set up and cash the additional tricks.

As the last part of the planning process, try to anticipate trouble. Many I/N players don't plan at all. You'll be a leg up on them when you do. The non-planners find themselves with a problem after a few tricks and then try to figure out how to fix it. Often it's too late. You'll be a giant step ahead of other I/Ns if you try to anticipate where things might go wrong with your plan. It's also important to remember that even though you have a plan, something during the play may cause you to change your approach. If something happens to surprise you, stop and decide whether your plan still works or whether you need a new one.

Here's a deal where you get to play a slam. (Some players find slams intimidating; actually, in some ways they're easier than partscores. When you can only lose one trick, you have far fewer options to choose from!) You are South, your side bids to 6♡ and after West leads the ♠J, you analyze your chances.

```
        ♠  K Q 2
        ♡  K Q
        ◇  A K Q 9 5
        ♣  9 5 2
        [                ]
        ♠  A 6
        ♡  A J 6 5 4 3
        ◇  7 4
        ♣  K 8 3
```

Following Declarer Device #1, you plan your play. It's a suit contract so you want to count your losers. None in spades; none in hearts, unless there is a 5-0 break; no diamonds; three possible club losers. However, once you draw trumps you can pitch two club losers on a good spade and good diamond. Six should be a piece of cake. Right?

Right, but can anything other than a 5-0 trump split sink our ship? What about a 4-1 trump split? You have the top four trumps, so as long as you clean out their trumps first you can still secure your contract by pitching the two losing clubs on the good spade and diamond and letting East-West take their ♣A.

Okay, with that resolved, you begin your play. Where are you taking the first trick? If you answered 'in hand with the ♠A', you're going down if trumps split 4-1. Following the plan to draw trumps, you'll lead a low trump to the ♡K, cashing the ♡Q next and finding out the bad news about trumps when East shows out on the second heart trick. No problem. Just get back to your hand to finish drawing trumps, right?

And how are you going to do that? You could ruff the third spade, but you need that winning spade trick to dump one of the clubs. How about taking the ◇AK and leading a small diamond to ruff?

Here's the full deal:

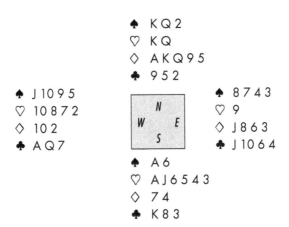

```
                    ♠ K Q 2
                    ♡ K Q
                    ◇ A K Q 9 5
                    ♣ 9 5 2
   ♠ J 10 9 5              ♠ 8 7 4 3
   ♡ 10 8 7 2              ♡ 9
   ◇ 10 2                  ◇ J 8 6 3
   ♣ A Q 7                 ♣ J 10 6 4
                    ♠ A 6
                    ♡ A J 6 5 4 3
                    ◇ 7 4
                    ♣ K 8 3
```

If you try to get back to your hand with a diamond ruff and trump low, West overruffs and cashes the ♣A for down one. If you ruff high so West can't overruff, you promote his ♡10 to a trick, and you are still going down one.

The way to make this 'gimme' contract is to plan all the way through the play before calling the first card from dummy. That includes any transportation issues you may have if bad things, like a 4-1 trump split, happen. If you do that, you'll decide to take the first trick in dummy and keep the ♠A as an entry to your heart length. If hearts don't break 3-2, you can use the ♠A to return safely to your hand and cash the ♡AJ to finish drawing trumps.

So perhaps we need a corollary to Declarer Device #1: *Plan your play — including determining what entries you need.*

By the time you get through this book you will have read 'plan first, play second' a lot of times. If you apply it on every deal, you'll save yourself a lot of misplayed hands.

## DECLARER DEVICE #2:
### Length makes strength.

Often the key to making a contract is to score tricks from a suit with length. Anyone can take tricks with aces and kings, so to be a winner you need to get those fives and sixes working hard for the cause.

Here's a deal from an Internet game I played with Denise Hoffman where suit length was crucial to making the contract. With both sides vulnerable, I was lucky enough to be dealt nine solid clubs, and we ended in a 5♣ contract with Denise as declarer. (Don't ask how Denise got to play this hand. Suffice it to say I was learning the Gambling 3NT convention at the time and was in step 3.5 — bidding it when I shouldn't.)

West leads the ♠K and South sees the following cards between dummy and her hand.

```
      ♠  9
      ♡  9
      ◇  A J
      ♣  A K Q J 9 8 5 4 2
      ▭▭▭▭▭▭
      ♠  6 5
      ♡  J 10 6 5 4
      ◇  7 5
      ♣  10 7 6 3
```

So let's play along with Denise. Remembering to plan first and play second, you look over the hand and immediately realize drawing trumps will not be a major problem. Because of North's distribution, counting the losing tricks from the perspective of dummy makes sense. Most frequently you should use this **dummy reversal** approach when dummy has more trumps than declarer. That's certainly the case with this deal and this is the way to think about this contract since it is easier to count losers from dummy's perspective. You find three losers: one each in spades, hearts and diamonds for down one, unless you can find a parking spot for one of them. There is one possibility, but it requires a little cooperation from your opponents.

Figure it out?

The only place the losing ◇J can go is on a good heart, if you can create one. If the defenders' hearts split 4-3 you may be able to ruff enough times that your fifth heart becomes a winner (there are other possibilities too, but they are much less likely, so let's ignore them for purposes of this discussion). Okay, we have a plan of sorts. Back to the play.

East, on a mission, overtakes West's ♠K with the ♠A and plays the ♡A (the bit of help you needed) taking their last trick and (as the cards lie) giving you the contract. As it happens, East is sitting with the ◇K and doesn't dare lead that suit in case you have the queen, so exits with the ♠J, which you ruff in dummy.

To lead hearts you have to be in your hand, and you have four entries in clubs because you ruffed the spade with a *high* club. You did do that, right? Once again, a key to planning your play is to account for necessary transportation between your hand and dummy. You must conjure enough entries to execute your plan.

So you lead the ♣2 now, overtake with the ♣3 and play a small heart, intending to ruff it. Both opponents follow suit and neither the king nor queen falls. So far, so good. Remembering to trump the heart trick high in dummy, you return to your hand by overtaking the ♣4 with your ♣6 and lead another heart, again ruffing high in dummy. Both opponents follow (yippee, a 4-3 split). After cycling clubs back to your hand once more and ruffing the fourth heart, you return to your hand for the final time by overtaking the ♣9 with the ♣10. Then you lead the sole remaining heart, discard the ◊J from dummy and claim the rest of the tricks, which is exactly what Denise did.

The keys to making this contract were your length in hearts (five headed by the J-10) and the four entries (in clubs) you created in your hand by making sure to trump everything high in dummy. Since hearts split 4-3 (which you can expect about two-thirds of the time), even if your heart holding had been ♡65432, you would have made the contract after the play to the first three tricks. That's the power of length.

We'll return to this deal in Chapter 3 and see how East-West could have set Denise using a technique we are about to discuss. Sometimes length isn't enough; the only way a contract makes is if the right opponents hold the right cards, in which case you need to follow…

## DECLARER DEVICE #3:
### Visualize necessity.

If the only way to make a contract is for your LHO to hold the stiff ♡K, play the hand as though he does and lay down your ♡A, fully expecting the ♡K to drop. If it doesn't, you were going down anyway, but sometimes your play works and you make an 'impossible' contract.

I had heard about 'placing' cards in other players' hands that had to be there for me to make the contract, but I didn't really understand the technique and how to apply the power of using my imagination until I read Mike Lawrence's *How to Read Your Opponents' Cards*. The book has lots of other useful material, but the biggest difference in immediately improving my game was that it got me starting to *visualize necessity*.

Let's look at an example of what I mean. Sitting South you sort this wonderful collection

♠A J 5   ♡A K   ◊A 7   ♣A Q 10 9 8 4

East passes, you open 2♣ with 22 HCP and a six-card club suit. The bidding proceeds as shown below and you end up playing a 3NT contract.

| West | North | East | South |
|------|-------|------|-------|
|  |  | pass | 2♣ |
| pass | 2◊[1] | pass | 3♣ |
| pass | 3♡ | pass | 3NT |
| all pass |  |  |  |

1. A positive bid showing at least an ace or a king or two queens.

West quickly slides the ◇Q onto the table. Plan your play.

♠ K 8 3 2
♡ J 6 5 3
◇ 8 6 4
♣ 3 2

♠ A J 5
♡ A K
◇ A 7
♣ A Q 10 9 8 4

Against notrump contracts, the lead of a queen usually asks partner to play the jack if she has it and otherwise give count. The leader will have something like KQ109x(x) in the suit for such a lead. Alternately, the lead could be from the top of a sequence like QJ10x(x)(x). Your opponents know what they are doing, so if East shows up with the ◇J, figure West for a lot of good diamonds once you take your ace.

Counting the tricks off the top, you have only six: two each in the majors and the aces of diamonds and clubs. You'll need to find three more tricks at a minimum. You can take a club finesse — but only once given dummy's puny clubs and only one possible entry to dummy, the ♠K.

Realistically, clubs is the only suit where you might find the extra tricks. Once you drive out the ♣K and ♣J, you can score the needed tricks. Except in the unlikely event that East has the doubleton king-jack, you still have to lose the lead in clubs at least once even if the finesse works. If West gets in, he'll bring down the contract with his diamonds. Therefore, you must assume either that the finesse works or that West has a singleton king that drops if you play the ace. You are missing five clubs. The chances of West having the singleton king are remote. Better to visualize East holding the king with an extra club or two or even three. You also need to visualize West not holding ♣Jxx because with that holding West will score the jack.

So necessity requires West to hold no better than Jx in clubs. However, the whole club analysis may be moot if East still has a diamond left after you take your ace. Then whichever opponent wins a trick in clubs, the rest of the diamonds are crammed down your throat. All righty then, time to play some cards and find out something about the diamond split. You call for a diamond from dummy. East complies with West's request and drops the ◇J. Continuing your plan to try to void East in diamonds, you play low.

West continues diamonds with the ◊K and East plays the ◊2. Either East is out of diamonds (the more likely scenario given the opening lead) or West started with four. If West started with four (the KQ109), you can bring the contract home if you can hold your club losers to one — and you don't care to whom you lose it since East-West can only score three diamond tricks in total. It's better to assume the worst and treat West as the dangerous hand.

Is it time to head over to dummy with the ♠K and take a club finesse? Out of necessity the club finesse must work, but is that the safest course? As you may have guessed, it is not. Suppose you use the ♠K as transport to dummy and lead a club, and the finesse wins. (You would stick in the queen, not the ten, since you must keep West off lead.) Now what? You are left playing clubs from hand. If East has ♣KJxx, you lose two club tricks and if East starts pushing spades through your ♠AJ, you have only one stopper left and West will get in if he has the queen.

No, we visualized that East must have the ♣K and West must not have ♣Jxx. Given those necessities, there is no reason not to give East his club trick or tricks in a way that doesn't further jeopardize the contract. Play the ♣A (which takes care of the rare case where West has a singleton king). Both opponents play low. Now play the ♣Q to trap a doubleton jack should West hold it.

Here are all four hands:

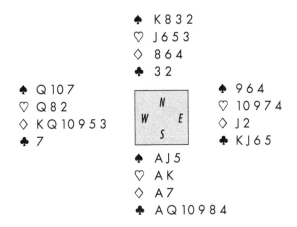

```
              ♠ K 8 3 2
              ♡ J 6 5 3
              ◊ 8 6 4
              ♣ 3 2
  ♠ Q 10 7              ♠ 9 6 4
  ♡ Q 8 2        N      ♡ 10 9 7 4
  ◊ K Q 10 9 5 3  W  E  ◊ J 2
  ♣ 7           S      ♣ K J 6 5
              ♠ A J 5
              ♡ A K
              ◊ A 7
              ♣ A Q 10 9 8 4
```

West shows out on the second club. East gets two club tricks, but try as he might, he can't find a way to West's good diamonds because you have double stoppers in both hearts and spades.

Length and visualization are great Devices, but they are not the only ones you need in your toolbox. Sometimes you have to score your honors, so let's look at the best way to do that.

## DECLARER DEVICE #4:
### Don't lead your honors, lead toward them.

Ever been in the situation where you lead your jack toward dummy's AQ combination, your LHO pops up with the king, you cover it with the ace and you think to yourself, 'darn', while showing your opponents your blank 'can't-read-what-I'm-thinking' face? Why 'darn'? Didn't you want the king to be in front of your ace so you could capture it? Yes, but... Let's look at a deal from an online tournament I played in. I was sitting North and my partner got to play a 4♡ contract.

West led the ◊A and these were the hands. Plan your play before continuing to read.

```
        ♠ J 7 6 5
        ♡ A Q 6 3
        ◊ 7 4
        ♣ K 7 6
        ┌──────────┐
        └──────────┘
        ♠ K Q 9 3 2
        ♡ J 8 5 4 2
        ◊ 5
        ♣ A 5
```

After winning the first trick West continued with the ◊Q, which my partner ruffed with the ♡2. No reason not to clear out trumps before East-West get an undeserved ruff somewhere. Many I/Ns would choose to lead the ♡J toward dummy's ♡AQ. If West goes up with the ♡K, dummy takes the trick with the ♡A. If West ducks, they'll let the ♡J ride, and if East doesn't take the trick they'll lead another heart toward the ♡AQ.

Duck soup — nothing easier, they think.

Let's imagine the possible hands East-West could have and see what happens when South leads either the ♡J or the ♡4.

What if trumps are split with West holding the singleton ♡K and East ♡1097?

When South leads the ♡J, West must play the ♡K, which dummy covers with the ♡A, East dropping the ♡7. Declarer can cash the ♡Q, but after that, East's ♡10 is promoted to top dog and will win a trick.

If South leads the ♡4, the ♡K still plops out of West's hand like a Thanksgiving turkey ready for the cranberry sauce, and the North-South ♡Q and ♡J will cover East's two hearts for no lost tricks.

I hear you saying, 'Yeah, but Jim, how likely is that?' Only around a 6% chance — not much, *but it's way more than 0%*. And those percentages make a big difference over time. The point is that leading the jack gives you no advantage and in some cases is a disadvantage. Learn to lead *toward* your honors and you'll score more of them.

Here's the whole deal:

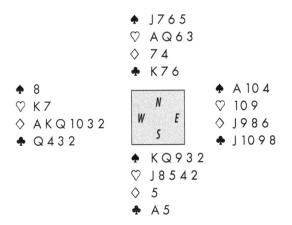

```
              ♠ J765
              ♡ AQ63
              ◇ 74
              ♣ K76
♠ 8                            ♠ A104
♡ K7          N                ♡ 109
◇ AKQ10032   W   E             ◇ J986
♣ Q432        S                ♣ J1098
              ♠ KQ932
              ♡ J8542
              ◇ 5
              ♣ A5
```

In this case, it didn't matter. Since you don't know ahead of time that you have a 'whatever-you-do-works' hand, make the percentage play. In other suit combinations it can make a big difference. Look at this situation, where you are missing the king:

$$QJ4$$

$$A752$$

Assume you need three tricks out of this combination and you have entries in other suits to use for transportation between hands. I can tell some of you are still skeptical about this 'leading toward an honor stuff'. Go ahead, put the queen's head on the guillotine and watch it roll after you lead Her Majesty. If East covers, she's dead and you win the trick with the ace. The jack can take a second trick; but only if the suit breaks 3-3 will you get the third trick. (That's only a fair chance, happening 36% of the time.) If West has the king you again lose the queen and still have the same 36% chance of a 3-3 split. So regardless of who has the king, if you lead your queen or jack toward the ace to take the finesse you have only a 36% chance to score three tricks and your honor is always eligible for a state funeral.

You improve your chances if you lead the deuce toward the queen. If East has the king, he'll take your queen. You'll still have the same 36% chance to score three tricks. *But*, if West has the king and plays it, you have three tricks set up: the ace, queen and jack. If West does not play the king and your queen scores, return to your hand in another suit and lead the five toward the jack. West has the same problem: regardless of when he decides to take his trick, he gets one and you get three. Summarizing: if West has the king, you have 100% chance of scoring three tricks. Leading small toward the queen-jack gives you a good likelihood of success, with an overall probability of 68%. Now that's a *big* difference!

If we change the ace in hand to a king, the same principle applies:

Q J 4

[ ]

K 7 5 2

At first blush it seems to hardly matter; you are going to lose one trick to the ace. Okay, let's try this: lead the deuce toward the queen-jack. If West goes up with the ace, you score three tricks.

If West plays low and dummy's queen holds, come back to your hand in another suit and lead the five toward the jack. If West has a singleton or doubleton ace (not very likely, but it does happen about 10% of the time), playing this way scores three tricks even though the suit does not split 3-3 because West has to play his ace *before you play your honor*. If East has the ace, you are left with your 36% chance at a 3-3 break.

Notice you should lead toward the queen-jack combination, not toward the king, because you can repeat the lead to the queen-jack. If you lead toward the king and East ducks the first time, you have nothing left in your hand to lead toward, whereas you can lead up to the queen-jack twice.

Let's look at a deal from a club game. Sitting South with me as your partner, you are not vulnerable, but your opponents are. The bidding proceeds:

| West | North | East | South |
|------|-------|------|-------|
|      |       | pass | 1NT   |
| pass | 2◊[1] | pass | 2♡    |
| pass | 4♡    | all pass |    |

1. Transfer.

West leads the ◊10 and dummy is tabled:

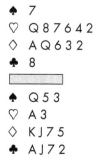

♠ 7
♡ Q 8 7 6 4 2
◊ A Q 6 3 2
♣ 8

[ ]

♠ Q 5 3
♡ A 3
◊ K J 7 5
♣ A J 7 2

As North, with wonky distribution and 8 points, I wanted us to be in game opposite your 1NT opening. Naturally, I caught you with only two hearts.

Since dummy has more trumps than declarer, let's count losers from dummy's point of view. With one loser in spades and none in diamonds or clubs, you need to hold heart losers to two tricks to make the contract.

How do you plan to do that?

Here's what happened at the table: South won the diamond lead in dummy with the ace, and led the ♡Q. East played the ♡10, declarer the ♡3 and West took it with the ♡K. West cashed the ♠A, led a diamond and discovered East was out of diamonds and (fortunately, in one way, from declarer's perspective) was also out of trumps. Unfortunately, West held ♡J95 behind declarer's ♡A and claimed two heart tricks. 'Bad break,' everyone else at the table said and recorded the score. Remembering Declarer Device #4 — *Don't lead your honors, lead toward them* — I was a bit skeptical of the play. (And given the topic under discussion you should be *very* skeptical!)

The key to this deal is to hold the trump losers to two and ensure East-West can't trump your diamonds, since without the intervention of magic you have no way to get rid of the spade loser.

Let's isolate the heart suit:

♡  Q 8 7 6 4 2

♡  A 3

If hearts split 3-2 it's a gimme — at worst you win the ace and they score the other two tricks. What if they don't split 3-2? If hearts are 5-0, you are going down — they get at least three tricks. How about a 4-1 split? You are missing the KJ1095. Can you make it if the KJ109 are in one hand? If they are in East's hand, you're toast — they collect three tricks. However, you can arrange to lose only two heart tricks if they are in West's hand.

♡  Q 8 7 6 4 2

♡  K J 10 9                                     ♡  5

♡  A 3

Capture the opening diamond lead in your hand. Following the general rule to lead toward honors, you lead the ♡3 toward the ♡Q. If West ducks (and generally he should) you score your ♡Q. Then play a low heart to your ♡A. The opponents only get two hearts and a spade. If West does go up with the ♡K on the first heart lead, the next two heart tricks are yours with the ♡A and ♡Q; they'll get one more heart trick and the spade.

Can anything go wrong with this approach?

Yes. If East has a singleton ♡K, you will lose three heart tricks. Well, don't you just hate it when you lose a trick to a singleton king? I sure do, but it is four times more likely that the king is in the hand with four trumps than that it's a singleton.

Anything else?

Yes. Hearts break 3-2 and West hops up with the ♡K, cashes the ♠A and leads another diamond, which East ruffs. Expletive deleted.

Can *anything* solve the problem?

Yes. Cash the ♡A first (which also takes care of the singleton king problem) and lead a low heart toward the ♡Q. If trumps are 4-1 and West pops up with the king, your ♡Q is good and West gets only one more trump trick. If West hops up with the king and gives East a diamond ruff, trumps split 3-2 and you make anyway.

Eureka! An approach to take care of all 3-2 trump splits as well as 4-1 splits where West has KJ109, or where one hand has a singleton king. I'm not going to go into all the other possible four-trump holdings — trust me when I tell you that playing the ace and then leading a small heart toward the queen works in twice as many scenarios than starting off by leading the queen from dummy. Of course if the opponents bid, you would take any inferences into account in planning your play.

So now we've got this puppy nailed down. But can you do this kind of analysis while sitting at the table? Maybe you can, but I sure can't. For best results in situations like this, just follow Declarer Device #4: cash the ace to take care of the unlikely singleton king, and then lead low toward the queen.

Gosh, isn't this fun?

Here's the full deal:

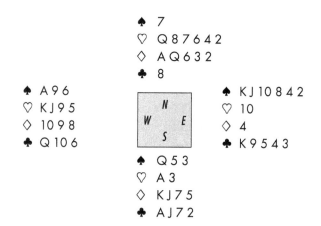

```
                    ♠  7
                    ♡  Q 8 7 6 4 2
                    ◇  A Q 6 3 2
                    ♣  8
  ♠  A 9 6                              ♠  K J 10 8 4 2
  ♡  K J 9 5          N                 ♡  10
  ◇  10 9 8       W       E             ◇  4
  ♣  Q 10 6           S                 ♣  K 9 5 4 3
                    ♠  Q 5 3
                    ♡  A 3
                    ◇  K J 7 5
                    ♣  A J 7 2
```

Since there is no reason to expect East to have four hearts, you should take the standard approach on this deal. As the cards lie, when you play the ♡A and lead low to the ♡Q, you'll hold your heart losers to two and make the contract.

Let's look at one more combination.

A Q 10 3

K 9 5 2

This time, you need four tricks and are missing the jack. If the suit is 3-2 you can take them from the top, but you know nothing about the suit distribution. You have a two-way finesse if you need it, but even with all that firepower, you can't guarantee the contract without peeking. However, if the split is 5-0, you are home free like this: lead low to the AQ (the hand with the double high honor). If LHO shows out, take the ace, then the queen, and lead low toward your K9, trapping the jack and scoring four. Otherwise, play the ace and if RHO shows out, lead low to the king. Now lead low toward the Q10, again trapping the jack.

Okay, 3-2 and 5-0 are a breeze (when did you last hope for a 5-0 split?). How do you play against a 4-1 split? Try everything in your power before you play the suit to figure out which opponent might have the four. To the extent you can, play off the other suits to try to get the count. Heck, ask; maybe they'll tell you.

If all else fails, you can safely lead low to the ace and see which cards they play. Remember, by playing first toward the hand with the double high honors, you keep your chances alive for finessing in either direction and scoring all your tricks if a 5-0 split appears. If the jack doesn't fall and they both play low cards, you'll have to guess whether to cash the queen or lead toward the king.

There are many more suit combinations you can try out on your own to increase your feel for best play when missing honors, but keep in mind that leading toward your honors is the key ingredient to success.

## DECLARER DEVICE #5:
### Give the opponents the chance to mess up —
### never do their work for them.

It's tough for Type A 'driving' bridge players to lay back and see what develops. We want to force the action, but sometimes waiting is the best policy.

Here's an example. Everyone is vulnerable, and you and I are sitting South. (Okay, I was sitting South; you can choose to stand up if you think this one isn't going to work out well.) In a contested auction I won the contract at 2♡, which West doubled. You'll notice I didn't show the bidding on this deal. My bid was terrible and I wouldn't make it today, but that's another story.

Here's the full deal so you can follow along with my thinking one trick at a time:

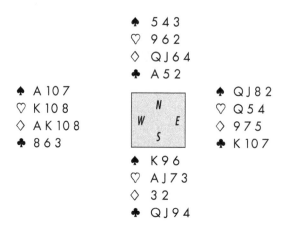

```
                    ♠ 5 4 3
                    ♡ 9 6 2
                    ◇ Q J 6 4
                    ♣ A 5 2
   ♠ A 10 7                        ♠ Q J 8 2
   ♡ K 10 8           N            ♡ Q 5 4
   ◇ A K 10 8     W       E        ◇ 9 7 5
   ♣ 8 6 3           S            ♣ K 10 7
                    ♠ K 9 6
                    ♡ A J 7 3
                    ◇ 3 2
                    ♣ Q J 9 4
```

West leads the ♡8, dummy is displayed and I start counting losers — way too
many losers. They can make 2♡, not me. I can easily go down three for -800. (I
had obviously not fully learned my lessons on when and how to compete in the
bidding.) Oh well — nothing to do but play it out and apologize to partner later.
I duck the heart lead in dummy, East ducks too (not a good decision) and I win
with the ♡J.

Trick 2: I try to set up dummy's ◇QJ while I still have a club entry by leading
the ◇2 toward the honors (Declarer Device #4). West goes up with the ◇K, dummy
and East play small.

Trick 3: West leads the ♡K, which I duck. With the ♠K in my hand, I'm
happier with West having the lead.

Trick 4: Rather than shift and try to knock out my club entry in dummy, West
continues trumps. I win with the ♡A, breathing a small sigh of relief when hearts
split 3-3.

Trick 5: I continue my plan and lead the ◇3 toward the ◇QJ. West ducks this
time (the ♣A is an entry to the ◇QJ if he goes up with the ◇A). I call for the ◇Q
from dummy and it holds.

Trick 6: Based on the bidding and play, it is extremely unlikely that a singleton
♣K is going to fall if I lead the ♣A. I lead a low club (again remembering to lead
low toward honors), leaving the ♣A as an entry to what could be a good diamond
if an opponent tries to cash the ◇A. East ducks and I take the trick with the ♣Q.

Trick 7: Thinking I know where the ♣K is, I shift plans and lead a small club
to the ♣A; East and West both play low.

Trick 8: I give up a club trick to East's ♣K, knowing I'll get the heart trick and
the good ♣J. By golly, I can even make the contract if East has the ♠A.

Here are the remaining cards:

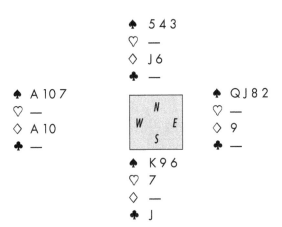

Trick 9: Logically, East should lead the ♠Q (in fact, any spade will do in this layout) and I would go down for a richly deserved bad score (though not as bad as I really deserved). Instead, he leads the ◊9 to West's good ◊A. I pitch a small spade.

Trick 10: West is cooked. A diamond lead gives me the ◊J as my sixth trick, and I still have a good trump and the ♣J to make eight. If he leads a spade, it sets up my ♠K. He cashes the ♠A.

Tricks 11-13: West leads another spade and I score the ♠K. The heart and club are good, and I make the contract.

Through a series of gaffes my opponents allowed me (and you too if you did decide to stick with me on this one) to make the doubled 2♡ contract. I could have pressed the issue and one of the times I was in dummy led toward my ♠K to score it if East held the ♠A. It's a 50/50 chance, and the bidding and play didn't tell me enough to let me guess which hand held the ♠A. But why do the opponents' work for them? The ♠A is wherever it is. If I don't lead spades they must. If I'm really lucky West will have to lead up to me, guaranteeing the ♠K scores a trick.

I hasten to add that you shouldn't count on the opponents messing up the defense as much as they did in this deal. However, this patience thing can really work out well sometimes.

## DECLARER DEVICE #6:
### Not all finesses must be taken.

Before I saw the light, if I encountered a finesse opportunity I was drawn to it like a moth to flame. I was what Eddie Kantar calls a 'Finessaholic'. I'd take any finesse as soon as possible — might as well know if it worked, I figured. Now I take a finesse only if I must.

Deciding if and when to take a finesse is all about working the odds in your favor. Sometimes the opponents are very helpful and lead into your AQ tenace — sometimes they are extremely kind and do it with their opening lead. When that happens, smile to yourself and sing hosannas. Not all your opponents will be so obliging, so let's talk about how to deal with hands where your opponents don't giftwrap the solution to your problem of whether or when to finesse.

Some situations are easier than others. When should you finesse with this combination?

K J 7 2

A 9 8 6 5 4 3

Never. I'm sure you got this one right — you have an eleven-card suit. The worst the suit can split is 2-0. Play your ace and king in any order you please and the queen and ten either both fall on the first trick or one each on the two tricks.

Okay, that was pretty easy. How do you play this next combination, assuming neither opponent bid and, for whatever reason, you must play this suit first, so you can't gain any additional information? For simplicity, let's assume the suit is trumps.

A 8 4 3

K J 10 7 5 2

I'll bet you counted the cards and came up with ten, leaving the opponents the Q96. All three cards could be in either hand, or they could split 2-1. If you knew they were 2-1, then you could play your ace and king and collect all their trumps. If you knew East had all three trumps, it would be easy to finesse the queen and score all three tricks. But you don't know. You asked them nicely, but they wouldn't tell you!

One approach is to cash the ace and see what happens. If trumps split 2-1, then cash your king and move on. If East has all three cards, you are in dummy and can immediately finesse against the queen and bring the suit home. If West has all three, you are going to lose a trick. 'Oh, but I always finesse against West,' I hear you say, 'and that would have worked' — until, of course, I put all three cards in East's hand and then you took the finesse the wrong way.

Cashing the ace and only finessing if West shows out nearly always wins all the tricks — 89% of the time. Certainly better than a 50/50 guess off the top, which is what it would be if you just close your eyes and take the finesse.

However, you can also apply Declarer Device #5 — *Give your opponents the chance to mess up* — and bait your hook with a juicy worm. Sometimes you get a fish to bite. Because you also have the ten, you can lead the jack from your hand. West might decide to cover your jack, either from a mistaken understanding of the 'rule' to cover an honor with an honor, or because he might hope to promote something in his partner's hand. It is not your intention to take the finesse, but West may not know that, and you are offering him the opportunity to solve your problem and pop up with the queen. If he doesn't, you are no worse off because you are going to play the ace in any event. But if he does give up the queen from Q96, you've scored a trick you didn't deserve and that's always a good thing.

As an aside, how did I know your chances of picking up their trumps were 89%? In Appendix B (page 162) is a list of the probabilities of some of the more common suit splits. On my road to becoming a Life Master I realized I was making poor decisions because I did not know these probabilities. I used my flashcard method to memorize them. You could do the same or simply study the charts to understand the basic rules. In general, with an odd number of cards outstanding, the closest split to even has the highest probability, and the probabilities tail off from there. When there are an even number of cards outstanding, an even split is less likely than one off from even. For example, with six cards missing, a 3-3 split occurs roughly 36% of the time and 4-2 occurs 48%. Interestingly, for two cards missing, the 1-1 split is slightly more likely than 2-0 (52% to 48%).

If you fondly remember probability and statistics from your schoolwork, you can search the internet and find several websites that will provide you with the exact formulae. For the rest of us, Appendix B can be a handy reference.

I'll bet you've heard the expression, 'eight ever; nine never'. When you have eight or nine cards in a suit including the ace and king but not the queen, the rule tells you whether to take a finesse (eight ever) or play for the drop (nine never). Even with the 'eight ever' part of the rule, there is a right way and a wrong way to play it.

Here's the right way. For simplicity, let's say you can only finesse against your RHO as in this position:

A 4 3 2

KJ 6 5

The first thing to do is cash the ace (the honor in dummy — use that one, otherwise you've given up your chance to finesse against RHO). If the queen happens to be a singleton, it drops on the first trick and you don't have to finesse, which is why you cash an honor first.

If the queen doesn't drop (and it rarely does) and both opponents follow suit, then take the finesse. Easy enough. How often will that strategy work? If you work through the math, it turns out that the success rate of playing the cards this way to capture the queen is almost 53% — a bit better than the 'intuitive' 50%. The 3% difference is the bonus you get for playing the ace first when LHO has the singleton queen. While that difference seems small, over time you will experience a big difference in your success if you manage your play to gather up those spare percentages for your side of the table.

So what happens if you try to drop the queen by playing the ace and king? You succeed only about 35% of the time. Clearly, cashing an honor and finessing for the queen when you have an eight-card suit is a much superior approach compared to trying for the drop.

How about the 'nine never' aspect of the 'rule'? Missing the queen and three small, your chances of dropping the queen are about 58%. Now let's look at what happens when you try the finesse. You know the percentage is greater than 50% because you will first cash an honor that captures a singleton queen. How much higher? This time the total is just over 56%. That's not a lot less than the 58% from the drop strategy. As you learn more advanced declarer skills, you will discover that other considerations (like not letting the dangerous opponent gain the lead) can be more important than the 2% gain you get with the drop strategy. However, with nothing else to guide you, play for the drop with nine cards in the suit.

Here's an example to try out your finessing skills. In uncontested bidding you arrive in a 3NT contract.

♠ 4 3 2
♡ 9 3
♢ A K 6 4 3
♣ 8 7 4

♠ A Q J
♡ A 6 5 4
♢ Q 7
♣ A K Q 2

West leads the ♡2. Counting winners, you have eight on top, and lots of chances for more. Clubs might break, diamonds might break (giving you two extra tricks!) and there's the spade finesse too. By the way, does it matter when you take your ♡A? A hold-up play can be advantageous if by holding up you are able to make the opponent who is shorter in the suit run out. That way, should she later gain the lead, she won't have a card to lead back to her partner so her partner can run the suit.

In this case, holding up is unlikely to do much good. Many people lead the fourth highest of their longest and strongest suit. The ♡2 tells a tale — West started with exactly four hearts, so (unless West is messing around) the defense will have three heart winners after you take your ace. And if the spade finesse loses, it's West (who has the long hearts) who is going to win that trick.

Did you decide on a line of play? Okay, let's watch declarer on this hand and see what happens. South ducks the first trick and takes the heart continuation. Now declarer tries clubs, which turn out to be 4-2. Carefully cashing the queen first, she plays off three top diamonds, but they are not friendly either. She's in dummy now for the spade finesse — but the king is offside. The defense take that, a couple more hearts and a trick declarer set up for them in the minors. How unlucky can you get? That contract was almost 80%, and yet still she went down.

Well, no. Actually that contract was 100%. Remember Declarer Device #6 that *not all finesses need to be taken*. The spade finesse here is a case in point — it's a mirage. Declarer started with eight top tricks, and by just conceding a trick to the ♠K, she could produce an easy ninth. All she had to do was win the ♡A whenever she felt like it, and play the ♠A and ♠Q. The defense would take their king, and declarer's ninth trick would be the ♠J.

Sometimes you can't avoid a finesse entirely, but you can postpone it to the last possible moment, making sure you try every other option first. That's what you should be thinking about on this next deal:

| West | North | East | South |
|------|-------|------|-------|
|      |       |      | 1♣    |
| pass | 1♡    | pass | 1NT   |
| pass | 3NT   | all pass |   |

Your RHO leads the ♠6, and dummy appears. Plan your play.

```
        ♠ J 5
        ♡ A Q J 7
        ◇ K 8 6 2
        ♣ A 7 6
        [_____]
        ♠ A 3
        ♡ 10 9 4
        ◇ A 5 4
        ♣ K J 10 9 3
```

Who has the ♣Q? Have you heard the expression, 'one peek is worth two finesses'? This is the kind of deal the wit who coined that phrase had in mind. But peeking is cheating. (And I know you're not going to flip ahead a page or two to see the full deal!) It's a notrump contract, so counting winners is the way to start. You have six: a spade, a heart, two diamonds and two clubs. You'll need to find three additional tricks to make your contract.

Let's see what the opening lead tells us. When someone makes a fourth-best lead, the number of higher cards in the other three hands is eleven minus the lead's spots (the **Rule of Eleven**). In this instance with the lead of the ♠6, you know North, East and South have a combined five cards higher than the ♠6. North has one, you (South) have one, which means East has three. Since East has three, it does no good to duck the first trick and hope to run East out of spades so he can't lead them back to West. He'll have at least one card left when you run out.

By the way, the opening leader's partner (East in this example) can also use the Rule of Eleven to determine how many higher cards in that suit declarer has. So East knows you have only one. (We'll talk more about the Rule of Eleven in Chapter 3.)

Of course, small card leads in notrump are not always fourth best. Sometimes the opponent chooses an opening lead to try to find a way to set up a suit he thinks partner has. This often happens when partner bids, but also occurs when the leader has no suit of his own to set up and he takes a stab at finding his partner's long suit. In this deal you can use the fact that neither opponent made a bid to analyze the spade situation, which brings us to:

## DECLARER DEVICE #7:
### Draw inferences from the bidding.

Whoa, Nellie, I can hear you say. I thought Chapter 1 was about bidding and this chapter about declarer play. Right you are. I didn't specifically include this tip in the bidding section because most I/N players already listen to the bidding while it's happening — but many of them forget all about the auction once it is over. Even if they do remember the actual bids, they often fail to take inference from the passes, which can be just as important.

On this deal, you and partner have 26 HCP, which means the opponents have 14. With nine spades outstanding, for East to have only two spades, West would have to have seven. If West had a seven-card spade suit and some of the missing points, you would expect him to preempt in spades after you opened. If East had the seven spades and some points, he would have bid spades after partner's 1♡ bid. Either way you look at it, their lack of bidding implies neither has a seven-card spade suit, and they will both have spades remaining after yours are but a fond memory.

It is always possible that West led from the KQxx(x), so there is no reason not to call for dummy's jack and possibly snare a gift trick. The only real reason to duck is to let East take the first trick and then hope East makes a terrible blunder and leads back a heart or a club to give you a free finesse. Those chances are someplace between slim and none. You play the ♠J, which East overtakes with the ♠Q.

After you take your ♠A, it's decision time and the stakes are high. If you lose the lead, your contract fails under a flood of spade tricks. You already learned that 'eight ever' is a good rule. You would apply it by cashing the ♣A and then finessing the ♣J (53% rather than a straight 50/50 shot since the ♣Q might fall when you cash the ♣A). However, your heart suit is missing the king and you do not have the luxury of being able to play the ace, hope for the king to drop, and still take the finesse. Hearts are therefore a straight 50% chance. So clubs it is. Right?

Clubs, yes; finesse, no! When we looked at 'eight ever, nine never' we analyzed the play considering the suit in isolation. Here we have two suits in which we can try to get our extra three tricks. Instead of taking a finesse in clubs, we should try for the drop in clubs by playing first the ace and then the king. You may recall that had only a fair chance of success (about 35%). But regardless of whether the drop fails or works, we still have the lead after the two tricks. If the ♣Q happens to drop we are golden because we can cash the remaining clubs and reach our nine-trick goal without taking the heart finesse.

The remaining 65% of the time the drop fails, but we can then try the heart finesse, which still has a 50/50 chance. By playing first the ♣A and then the ♣K we end up in the correct hand to take the heart finesse. This combination approach increases our overall odds from about 50/50 to the very good category of 67.5%. The combination approach is a huge improvement, increasing our chances of bringing in the contract by almost one-third compared to just taking the club finesse.

Since it doesn't matter what cards East-West had, I haven't bothered to waste space with the whole deal, which is why I knew for sure you wouldn't skip ahead to check out which finesse would win.

## DECLARER DEVICE #8:
### Draw trumps at the right time to guarantee the contract.

Let's look at a deal from an online tournament, but pretend it was played in a team knockout session. Sitting North, I drew

♠A 10 7 4  ♡10 7 6 5  ◇8  ♣A K Q 6

and opened 1♣. The bidding went as follows:

| West | North | East | South |
|------|-------|------|-------|
|      | 1♣    | 2◇[1] | 2♡   |
| 2NT  | 4♡    | all pass |   |

1. Preemptive.

West leads the ◇J and I lay down dummy. Plan your play with the North-South hands over the page before continuing to read.

$$\spadesuit \text{ A 10 7 4}$$
$$\heartsuit \text{ 10 7 6 5}$$
$$\diamondsuit \text{ 8}$$
$$\clubsuit \text{ A K Q 6}$$

$$\spadesuit \text{ 8}$$
$$\heartsuit \text{ K Q J 9 3}$$
$$\diamondsuit \text{ K 6 5 2}$$
$$\clubsuit \text{ 8 5 2}$$

You count your losers. With this lead, you should now score your ◊K, leaving four losers: three diamonds and a heart. You are going to have to ruff the diamonds in dummy, unless either clubs split 3-3, in which case you can pitch a diamond on the good ♣6, or by some magic (which never happens to me or my partners) the ♠10 becomes a winner and you can pitch a diamond on it.

Here's how the play actually proceeded. East took the first trick with the ◊A and led back a small spade. Dummy's ♠A overtook West's ♠J. Dummy led a small heart and East pitched a diamond. Trumps split 4-0, normally only a 10% chance. Aren't you the lucky one today? Of course, applying Declarer Device #7, after East made the preemptive 2◊ bid, followed by West's 2NT bid presumably showing a heart stopper, the bad trump split was almost a certainty on this deal. West let the ♡K hold, as well as the ♡Q, but hopped up with the ♡A to overtake the ♡J.

West finished the job of clearing trumps by leading his last heart, which declarer won in dummy, leaving the following position:

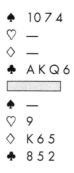

$$\spadesuit \text{ 10 7 4}$$
$$\heartsuit \text{ —}$$
$$\diamondsuit \text{ —}$$
$$\clubsuit \text{ A K Q 6}$$

$$\spadesuit \text{ —}$$
$$\heartsuit \text{ 9}$$
$$\diamondsuit \text{ K 6 5}$$
$$\clubsuit \text{ 8 5 2}$$

Cashing the top clubs, South discovered clubs broke 3-3. After scoring the last club and pitching a diamond, she ruffed a spade in hand, cashed the ◊K and conceded a diamond to East. Contract made, which, South figured, is the name of the game in IMP scoring.

When the team came together to compare scores, they discovered the other team made an extra trick on this deal, yielding a 1-IMP loss. Most team matches aren't won or lost by 1 IMP, and since this was an imaginary match anyway, we'll give our team an overall win with a comfortable margin overcoming the small loss on this deal. (If you are playing an imaginary match, I suggest you add three top pros to your team.) You might be wondering: was it poor defense by your teammates that caused the mishap or did South misplay her cards? Well heck, folks, we *are* in the declarer play section of this book...

Here's the whole deal:

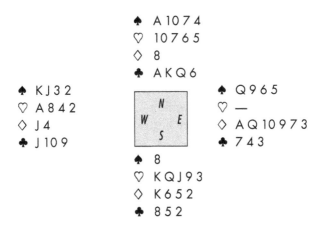

♠ A 10 7 4
♡ 10 7 6 5
◇ 8
♣ A K Q 6

♠ K J 3 2
♡ A 8 4 2
◇ J 4
♣ J 10 9

♠ Q 9 6 5
♡ —
◇ A Q 10 9 7 3
♣ 7 4 3

♠ 8
♡ K Q J 9 3
◇ K 6 5 2
♣ 8 5 2

So where did South drop a trick? In handling the trump suit — hearts. When declarer discovered on the first trump trick that hearts were 4-0, she needed to revise her plan on when to pull trumps. Take a look at the trump positions. West is going to score the ♡A for sure, but you have West's ♡842 covered.

Some I/N's religiously draw trumps as soon as they get in the lead. Others seem to have a phobia about drawing trumps. The first approach often works, but sometimes you need to make better use of dummy's trump suit. However, delaying drawing trumps risks the opponents ruffing your otherwise good tricks.

During the planning stage you should determine when to draw trumps. If you are not going to use dummy's trumps to ruff losers in your hand, the general rule is to draw trumps immediately. If you need to ruff tricks in dummy, make sure you will still have trumps available to do the job.

In this deal, after you win the second trick with the ♣A in dummy, you still have three losers: the ♡A, which you can do nothing about, and two diamonds, which you may be able to ruff in dummy. To guarantee the contract you must ruff one of the two diamond losers. To ruff a diamond you have to be in hand, and you can get there with hearts or spades. Which do you choose?

Since you do not need all four hearts in dummy for ruffing, it is generally safest to lead a heart. West let you win with the ♡K, and you discovered the 4-0 split. Now what?

Get the ruff now!

Yes, given East's 2◇ bid, West probably has two diamonds, and if so you can cash the ◇K safely before getting the diamond ruff. However, some Easts might bid 2◇ with a seven-card suit, in which case you make your life more complicated if West trumps your ◇K. I know you can overruff, but let's lead a low one anyway.

West plays the ◇4 and you ruff with a low heart. Now you can pull the remaining trumps including the ♡A, cash your good ◇K, cross over to dummy's good clubs and be pleasantly surprised when clubs break 3-3 and you make an overtrick, pitching the losing diamond on the good ♣6.

Why not ruff both losing diamonds and not rely on a 3-3 club break to make the overtrick?

Remember, the primary objective in a team game is to guarantee making the contract and go for overtricks only after you have assured success. If you try to ruff twice, you have problems with trump control. Let's follow the play if you try to ruff both losing diamonds. After ruffing the first diamond, you need to return to your hand to lead another diamond. How about hearts again? If you lead a heart from dummy, this time West wins the trick and leads another heart — no more ruffing power in dummy. Okay, how about leading a spade and ruffing in hand?

Back in hand you lead a diamond and West has choices. He can go up with the ♡A — but he always has that trick. Instead, he discards a club, hoping to ruff one of your good clubs. You get your second diamond ruff. If you lead a trump now, West wins with the ♡A and leads a spade, causing you to lose control of the hand. If instead you lead another spade and ruff again in hand, there is nothing left to do but try to cash the clubs. You only get two because West can now ruff the third club trick. You make your contract, but no overtricks.

You'll meet a similar fate if at Trick 3 you immediately lead a spade and ruff it in your hand with the ♡3. (Go ahead and try it if you want.)

Generally, when your play involves crossruffing (spades and diamonds in this example) you should cash your side winners first. But given the possible wonky distribution indicated by East's 2◇ bid, cashing the clubs before drawing trumps may be dangerous. It is certainly possible that East has a heart and only two clubs and will ruff a club if you haven't already drawn the trumps.

So utilize your trumps to guarantee your contract, and look for overtricks once you have guaranteed it.

## DECLARER DEVICE #9:
### Love the one you're with.

You can hardly believe your eyes as you gaze upon this one-loser hand

♠ A K Q J   ♡ A   ◇ A Q J 10 7 6 5 4   ♣ —

After your 2♣ opening, somehow partner hijacks the auction and places the contract in 6NT, with him as declarer. You seriously consider whether 7◊ might not be a better contract, but decide to trust your partner and pass. You prepare to lay down this monster as dummy when your LHO (forgetting that your partner bid the notrump, not you with the monster hand) leads the ♣A.

After the director explains to your partner her five options, she cheerfully decides to become dummy herself and let you play the hand. Such generosity.

♠ 10 9 8 7 6
♡ K Q
◊ 3
♣ K Q J 10 9

───────

♠ A K Q J
♡ A
◊ A Q J 10 7 6 5 4
♣ —

I have to admit, if I am declarer, my first reaction when dummy appears is not going to be wild enthusiasm for the 6NT contract. Unless the opponents can score a quick ruff, 6◊ and 6♠ both look to be cold contracts with the only possible loser the ◊K. If your thinking is running along the same lines then gently slap your wrist, pull out an old vinyl thirty-three and crank up the volume to Crosby, Stills & Nash's 'Love the One You're With'. (If you are a little younger than I, download the song onto your MP3 player.)

*You must concentrate on what is, not what could have been.* You might think diamonds and spades will play better, but you are in 6NT and you need to love this contract because for the next few minutes, it is the one you're with.

So take a deep breath (without your opponents noticing, of course — with luck they're still shaking their heads at their lead out of turn). You have no major-suit losers. With the ♣A lead, you have one definite club loser. You will need to bring in all the diamonds to rescue this contract, which means either the finesse works *and* the ◊K is doubleton (because you can only take the finesse once), or the ◊K is a singleton.

Neither alternative is all that likely, but the finesse has a much better chance, so you turn your thoughts to dummy entries. You have exactly zero of them at the get-go. If you pitch the ♡A on the first trick and *if* the opponents are so kind as to continue clubs or switch to a heart, you could enter dummy (pitching a diamond from hand), dump all your spades on dummy's winning clubs, drop five more diamonds on the now winning spades and have the ◊A available to take the last trick, making your contract.

That, however, is a fairy tale, so you plan for rational play on the opponents' part and assume after winning the ♣A, LHO will lead a spade. (A diamond lead would give you a free finesse.) You can temporize and cash your four spade tricks, but then you have no choice but to tackle diamonds. Since you need them all, you must *visualize necessity* and play the ◇A, knowing that the ◇K will fall, allowing you to run the rest of your diamonds and make the contract.

Since there is no reason not to give your opponents the chance to mess up, you pitch the ♡A from hand. As expected, LHO is finally on the ball and switches to a spade, which you win in hand. Might as well play off the spades. (Who knows, in a different fairy tale an opponent might accidentally discard the ◇K!) No fairy tales here, and after the spades run out you lay down the ◇A. The ◇K appears — loving the one you were with and visualizing necessity brings in the contract.

Here's the whole deal:

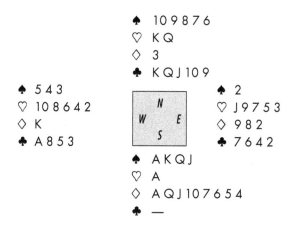

```
                    ♠ 10 9 8 7 6
                    ♡ K Q
                    ◇ 3
                    ♣ K Q J 10 9
  ♠ 5 4 3                          ♠ 2
  ♡ 10 8 6 4 2        N            ♡ J 9 7 5 3
  ◇ K            W         E       ◇ 9 8 2
  ♣ A 8 5 3           S            ♣ 7 6 4 2
                    ♠ A K Q J
                    ♡ A
                    ◇ A Q J 10 7 6 5 4
                    ♣ —
```

Although Declarer Device #9 — *Love the one you're with* — is the last tip on declarer play, it is a crucial step in helping you plan your play and execute it well. You need full concentration to be a darned good declarer and cannot afford for any of your brainpower to be sucked into what-might-have-beens.

Although you were lucky this time (wasn't I a nice guy?), it would be wise to make a note on your scorecard to discuss the bidding with partner after the session is over, since more often than not you will be down one in 6NT.

Let's end this chapter with a deal that utilizes many of the Declarer Devices. With North-South vulnerable, as South you pick up a hand with 1-4-4-4 distribution and 16 HCP:

♠ 5  ♡ K J 5 4  ◇ A K 6 4  ♣ A J 8 5

| West | North | East | South |
|------|-------|------|-------|
|      |       |      | 1♣    |
| 2♣[1] | 3♣   | 4♠   | 5♣    |
| 5♠   | 6♣    | all pass |    |

1. Showing 5-5 in the majors.

## Bidding Commentary:

West's 2♣ Michaels bid showed 5-5 in the majors (at least). Partner's 3♣ bid showed club support (should be at least five, since opener could have as few as three) and enough **support points** to be bidding at the three-level. East's jump to 4♠ is also preemptive, since it's clear they have a spade fit, but your side has the majority of the points. With a club fit, South's hand increases in value to 18 points because of the singleton spade. Even if partner has the ♣KQ, she's going to need more than that to make 5♣. However, since East-West seem to have most of the spades, it makes sense partner's points are in hearts and diamonds, so South bids game.

After West ups their sacrifice, North pushes to 6♣. Not exactly a scientific auction, but there you have it. West slides the ♠A onto the table and partner displays dummy. Plan your play and off you go.

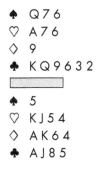

```
        ♠  Q 7 6
        ♡  A 7 6
        ◇  9
        ♣  K Q 9 6 3 2
        ┌──────────┐
        └──────────┘
        ♠  5
        ♡  K J 5 4
        ◇  A K 6 4
        ♣  A J 8 5
```

Trick 1: This is a no-brainer trick, but don't be tempted to call for the ♠6 from dummy until you plan your play. Clubs is clearly a good trump suit and six might even be the right contract. No matter; it's where you are and you *love the one you're with*. It's a suit contract so you count your losers: one spade, two hearts and two diamonds, totaling five. Often our initial reaction is to consider the play from the point of view of our own hand since we have more high cards (and are playing the contract). However, here dummy has the longer trump suit and under those circumstances, it may be more profitable to consider this contract using dummy reversal. From that perspective, you have three spade losers and one heart loser.

That's one fewer loser and when you consider how to handle those four losers, the way to making the contract becomes obvious. There is nothing to do about one spade loser, so concentrate on eliminating the other two spade losers and the one heart loser. You can, of course, take a finesse to try to score the ♡J, but given the bidding that seems unlikely to succeed. Besides, we've learned to avoid finesses when we can. Because of your singleton spade, you can ruff dummy's other spades, eliminating those two losers. You can also pitch a heart from dummy on the ◇K after you have taken the ◇A.

Gosh, this is looking quite doable. What can go wrong? Well, if you don't have two clubs left in hand to ruff the spades, your plan is trashed. You have ten trumps. If clubs break 2-1, you can immediately draw their trumps and not worry about nasty surprises. If trumps split 3-0, however, you can't afford to draw all their trumps because you won't have two left in hand to take care of the two spade losers. You are missing the ♣1074. With a 3-0 split and your honors split evenly between dummy and your hand, in order to avoid promoting the ♣10, you'll need to take at least one trump trick in your hand.

Any problems with entries? You need to get to dummy twice to lead the spades. You're in good shape with the ♡A and the ♣KQ. You can even ruff diamonds.

Anything else? Yikes! What if West made his Michaels bid with six hearts, and East has a heart void and a club to ruff with? You are not going to be a happy camper when on the second trick West switches to a heart, so *visualize necessity* and stick a heart in East's hand. With that minor adjustment you can breathe easier.

No other problems are rearing their ugly heads. Now you are ready to call for the ♣6 from dummy. East plays a discouraging ♣2, and you play your spade.

Trick 2: West considers dummy and while he's making his decision, despite your best efforts, the only thing you can think about is the possibility that East gets a heart ruff. West finally switches to the ◇3, gathering dummy's ◇9 and East's ◇10. You win the trick in hand.

Trick 3: In case trumps split 3-0, you play the ♣A to take the one trump trick you would need in hand. Good thing you did because West discards a low spade. East has all three clubs and you still need to make sure to avoid a heart ruff.

Trick 4: Lead a low club to dummy's ♣K. West pitches a small heart.

Trick 5: Lead a spade from dummy and ruff. East and West both follow.

Trick 6: You need to get back to dummy to lead the final spade, but how to get there? A club lead is safe, but doesn't leave anything to ruff the last spade with. When you planned your play, you visualized a heart in East's hand, so now you could lead a heart to the ace.

Don't do it! That visualization was necessary to save you from worrying about losing an early ruff to East's heart void. As soon as West led the diamond on Trick 2, you can cast aside your initial requirement that East have a heart. You need to replan to make the contract even if East has a heart void. Let West be the one to apologize for not finding his partner's void, not you for going down in a cold contract.

The safest way to dummy is to ruff a diamond. From the bidding, East should have at least five diamonds and may even have more. Lead a low diamond and trump low.

Trick 7: Dispose of dummy's last spade loser by ruffing it in hand with your last trump. East again follows.

Trick 8: East still has one trump outstanding and you need to pull it. Ruffing another diamond is still the safe way to dummy. Both opponents follow as you ruff.

Trick 9: Pull East's last trump with dummy's ♣Q. You pitch a low heart.

Trick 10: Lead a low heart to your ♡K.

Now play the ◊A, pitching a low heart from dummy. You still have the ♡A and a trump in dummy for the final two tricks. This time, East did have a heart, so your contract would have been safe if you had tried to use a heart to get to dummy, but next time you might not be so lucky. You formed a plan, reconsidered it when you discovered the unfortunate trump split and took a winning line of play. Well done.

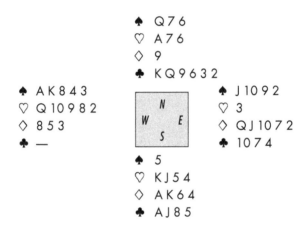

Of course there are many more things to learn about declarer play, but if you master the nine Declarer Devices in this chapter, you will score consistently higher than you did in the past.

Now let's turn to defense.

# Chapter 3:

# DECENT DEFENSE

Of the three main components of contract bridge — bidding, declarer play and defense — I/N players spend the least time studying defense. I have talked with lots of people about this, and I believe it happens because defense is the toughest part of the game. However, we can't just flop down our thirteen cards and wait for the next deal when we might get to be declarer. We bid on all the deals; we get to declare on only a quarter of the deals; we defend half of the time — twice as often as we declare.

A quarter of the time we are dummy while our partner is declarer. This means two-thirds of the time when we participate in the play, we are playing defense. We can't ignore defensive play and hope to do well.

I attribute much of my success during my I/N days to better-than-average defensive play, and I rate defense as the least developed part of my game. Where does that leave us? You will not become a great defender by reading this chapter, but by making the few easy changes to your game that I'm going to talk about, you can become a much better defender. Unlike declarer play, where you are on your own, in defensive play you also have your partner. To improve much of your defense you need your partner to be on the same wavelength.

Many of the Disciplines of decent defense will sound familiar, and indeed are identical to the Declarer Devices in Chapter 2. That's not surprising since declarer play and defense have much in common. The biggest difference is declarer's advantage because he knows all of his partnership's resources. As a defender you know half the defenders' and half the offenses' cards, and you can't control what your partner plays.

## DEFENSE DISCIPLINE #1:
### Plan first, then play.

Sound familiar? You or your partner leads and dummy comes down. At the same time declarer is planning how to make his contract, you should be planning how to defeat it. It isn't time to take a mini-nap when dummy hits the table. You both get to see twenty-six cards. Look at dummy and recollect the bidding, then try to figure out how declarer will attempt to make his contract and what you need to do to try to defeat his plan.

## DEFENSE DISCIPLINE #2:
### Draw inferences from the bidding.

Often the bidding provides you with a range of points for declarer. If declarer opened 1NT, you get the information directly. Sometimes the point range arrives indirectly: for example, declarer limited his hand by not jump-shifting, or showed 18-19 points by jumping to 2NT on his second bid.

The bidding also gives you clues about suit length. If declarer opened a major and did not rebid it when he had a chance, he probably has five rather than six cards in the suit.

Sometimes the bidding even shines a spotlight on their weak suit. If the opponents avoid going to notrump after bidding three suits, especially if they end up playing a 4♣ or 4◇ contract, you can bet it's because they don't have stoppers in the fourth suit.

Use declarer's thinking time as your thinking time and devise a plan or two before you play your next card.

If you can only change one thing about your defensive play, I suggest you concentrate on this one:

## DEFENSE DISCIPLINE #3:
### Agree on defensive carding.

The key method of communication between defenders is their carding. The information your carding conveys to partner differs depending on who is leading, your partner or the opponents. Entire books have been written on defensive carding. I am going to keep it simple here. Once you have mastered this chapter, treat yourself to a more advanced book on defensive play, but even applying the simple ideas in this book will put you a leg up on your I/N compatriots.

## DEFENSE DISCIPLINE #4:
### Know when to signal attitude, count and suit preference.

At the bottom left of the ACBL convention card (see Appendix A, page 160, if you're not familiar with it) it asks for your primary signal on partner's leads. If you are like most players in North America, check the box 'attitude'.

When your partner makes the opening lead you will play third to that trick. You will often have to play a high card to try to win the trick. However, if you can't win the trick (for example, your partner leads a small spade and dummy plays the ♠A) you need to tell your partner your attitude toward this suit. If you have the ♠K, you are keen to have him lead the suit again. If your highest spade is only the seven, spades is not a suit you are going to take a trick in, and you might prefer to suggest playing another suit. Assuming you have more than one spade, the spade you play will help your partner understand your attitude toward the suit.

In standard carding, playing the highest spade you can afford shows a positive attitude; your lowest spade shows a negative attitude. Sometimes you can't afford to signal with a high card because you hope to take a trick with that card. So you play a lower card, possibly misleading your partner (and probably declarer as well). This concern leads many players to choose 'upside-down' attitude signals. In the upside-down world, playing a low card is encouraging and playing a high card is discouraging.

If you would like to witness a stirring debate with no conclusion, get a group of world-class bridge players together and start a discussion about whether standard carding or upside-down carding is preferable. I witnessed such a discussion by a panel at a recent American Bridge Teachers' Association annual meeting. When the panel was asked the question, David Berkowitz (an upside-down proponent) stood and waved his hands around while suggesting strongly that high cards are for taking tricks. Much of the rest of the panel was unconvinced.

Since the experts don't agree, pick whichever works for you. For many, the standard 'high I like it, low I don't like it' method is more intuitive, and therefore works better. The important thing is to get good at signaling, regardless of what method you choose. In this book, we will use standard attitude and count signals unless a specific exception is noted.

Let's look at an example. Against a heart contract, your partner decides to lead the ◇3:

Dummy
◇ A Q 10

Partner's lead
◇ 3

You
◇ K J 9 2

If declarer doesn't play the ◇A from dummy, you are going to take the trick, which is fine but doesn't advance the lesson. Fortunately, declarer calls for the ◇A from dummy and graciously gives us a working example.

Before you can be sure you want to encourage partner, it helps to understand what kind of suit your partner might be leading from.

## DEFENSE DISCIPLINE #5:
### Play standard leads.

Let's take another look at an ACBL convention card (Appendix A). In the bottom left corner of the card the standard leads from different card combinations are indicated. Unless you and your partner have specific agreements otherwise, you should use standard leads. The bold type shows the standard card to lead from each holding. For example, against a suit contract it is standard to lead the king from KQx.

If your partnership does something other than what the ACBL considers 'standard', you need to circle it on your card. Notice the standard lead from three small against suit contracts is the smallest card. 'Boston' fans (**B**ottom **o**f **S**omething; **T**op **o**f **N**othing) need to circle the top 'x' since from three small cards they lead the highest one. If you're a fan of 'MUD' (**M**iddle **U**p **D**own), you lead the middle card from three small, so circle that one.

While experts debate about these three approaches (heck, they'll debate anything), most prefer to lead the lowest of the three to help partner get a count in the suit and make sure she doesn't try to give you a ruff. As with carding, unless specifically noted otherwise, we will assume standard leads.

Okay, let's get back to that diamond suit.

Dummy

◇ A Q 10

Partner's lead  You

◇ 3 ◇ K J 9 2

Before you can determine your attitude to partner's lead, you need to try to understand it. You hold the ◇2, so her lead is the smallest possible spot card. It could be a singleton, but that would mean declarer has six of them (and we'll assume he never bid them). Unlikely. It is not a doubleton for similar reasons, and anyway partner would have led the higher card. It's probably from three or four small cards. (You know where all of the honors are, so partner can only have small cards.) It could not be from five small cards because partner would have led her fourth highest from that holding, and there are no lower spots outstanding.

You conclude partner has three or four small diamonds. With three in dummy and four in your hand, it means declarer has two or three small diamonds. In either case you want to encourage your partner to lead the suit the next time she has the chance since you have the ◇KJ sitting over dummy's ◇Q10.

To signal your love of diamonds you play the ◇9, which is the highest diamond you can afford. You need the king and jack to cover dummy's cards, but those two cards also take care of any spot cards declarer has. Should you ever get to play your ◇2 on a fourth diamond trick, declarer will be out.

Easy, right?

Let's take another example. Again the opponents are playing a heart contract and partner leads the ◊3:

Dummy
◊ A Q 10 8

Partner's lead
◊ 3

You
◊ J 7 2

Dummy pops up with the ace. If declarer has the king, your jack is going to drop and he will end up with four diamond tricks after he has pulled trumps. The defense needs to find another suit to attack. You play the ◊2 to let partner know to pick a different suit next time she has the lead. So far, so good.

The third time is not the charm when everything is the same as the first example, except dummy's holding now includes the ◊8. Partner still leads the ◊3 and again declarer calls for dummy's ace.

Dummy
◊ A Q 10 8

Partner's lead
◊ 3

You
◊ K J 9 2

You go through the same thinking process as before. Depending on the exact bidding, it's possible that partner could be leading a singleton, in which case you should not be signaling attitude since she can't lead them again. But you don't know it's a singleton. Declarer could be the one with the singleton, in which case partner is leading low from four. Regardless of who has which diamonds, you would love to tell partner to lead them again when she has the chance. However, because of the cards you and dummy have, you can't afford to play anything other than the ◊2*. The bridge gods may not give you the perfect spot cards for the signal you want to make — you just have to hope partner can figure it out.

Remember, on the opening lead, your attitude signals to partner whether you want her to continue leading the suit or switch to a different suit.

Let's look at attitude signaling in the context of a whole deal — remembering to make a plan as early as possible. Only the opponents are vulnerable. With your side silent the bidding goes 1♡-2♣; 2♡-4♡. Your partner leads the ♠A (your partnership leads the ace from a suit headed by the ace-king). Dummy comes down and you consider your chances.

---

* This kind of situation is the rationale for 'upside-down' signals, which allow you to play the ◊2 here as an encouraging card. However, it's not hard to construct examples where that agreement gives you a similar problem, which is why experts disagree on which method is superior.

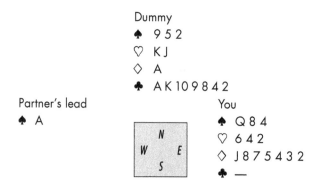

Dummy
♠ 9 5 2
♡ K J
♢ A
♣ A K 10 9 8 4 2

Partner's lead
♠ A

You
♠ Q 8 4
♡ 6 4 2
♢ J 8 7 5 4 3 2
♣ —

Putting aside your disappointment that despite your best attempts at mental telepathy, partner did not lead a club for you to ruff, you start to plan how to defeat the contract. Dummy has 15 HCP; credit declarer with at least 11 HCP and after reflecting your 3 HCP, that gives partner a maximum of 11. Subtract 7 for the ♠AK you now know partner has, and that leaves her with at most 4 other HCPs.

You and dummy have six spades, leaving seven between partner and declarer. Given the favorable vulnerability, you think partner would have bid 1♠ if he had five spades to the ace-king and even a useful outside queen. Even without an outside queen, she would have preempted with six spades. So either she doesn't have anything beyond the ♠AK and five spades or she has only four spades and too few points for a takeout double (or the wrong shape).

If partner has four spades, declarer has three and your side can garner three spade tricks off the top. If partner has five spades, then declarer has two and partner can win only one more spade with her ♠K. Any way you look at it, spades won't provide enough tricks to set the contract.

Wait. What if partner has four spades and the ♡A? Then the contract is going down; but I'm here to tell you, this time partner does not have the ♡A, and even if she did, you still have some defensive work to do because there are more tricks to be had.

You may collect a spade trick with the ♠Q, but the real defensive power of your hand is its club void combined with three available trumps. You like spades, but you want partner to switch to a club right now. You don't want her to cash the ♠K first. You want an immediate switch to collect your *first* ruff.

Why immediate? Because if she immediately gives you a club ruff, you can lead back to her ♠K and (as long as declarer has at least two clubs) you'll get a second ruff and set the contract. If declarer does have three spades, you can cash your ♠Q and set them two tricks.

To tell partner that you don't want her to continue spades, play your lowest spade, the ♠4. Does that guarantee she will switch to a club? Unfortunately, no. Often, given the bidding and dummy, it's clear to partner what suit you want led. This time, partner will go through the same analysis that you did when you determined the range of her possible HCPs. Because she has no information about your hand (other than that you never bid), she could speculate you might be sitting with the ◇K. Then if she has clubs stopped, she could convince herself that the best thing she can do is lead a heart to take potential ruffing power off the board.

Fortunately, she has several low clubs. When she sees dummy's seven clubs and your discouraging attitude toward spades, she figures the only way you two will defeat the contract is if you have a club void.

She switches to the ♣7, you get your ruff and lead back a spade. Partner takes that trick and leads back another club. You ruff the second club trick, cash the ♠Q, and declarer claims the rest for down two.

If you play the ♠8 on the first trick, partner will continue the ♠K and then a low one. She probably thinks she is giving you a ruff. You'll win the ♠Q and lead a low diamond to dummy's ace, hoping declarer will lead a club. No such luck. Here are the four hands.

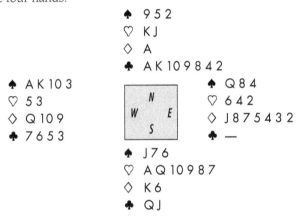

```
              ♠ 9 5 2
              ♡ K J
              ◇ A
              ♣ A K 10 9 8 4 2
♠ A K 10 3                      ♠ Q 8 4
♡ 5 3           N              ♡ 6 4 2
◇ Q 10 9     W     E            ◇ J 8 7 5 4 3 2
♣ 7 6 5 3        S              ♣ —
              ♠ J 7 6
              ♡ A Q 10 9 8 7
              ◇ K 6
              ♣ Q J
```

Let's look at another example where North-South bid to a heart game, this time with a 1♡-2♡-4♡ bidding sequence. Your partner leads the ♠K.

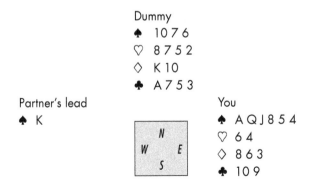

```
Dummy
♠ 10 7 6
♡ 8 7 5 2
◇ K 10
♣ A 7 5 3

Partner's lead                    You
♠ K                               ♠ A Q J 8 5 4
              N                   ♡ 6 4
           W     E                ◇ 8 6 3
              S                   ♣ 10 9
```

You have nothing other than spades, and you clearly want them led again. Which card do you play using standard attitude?

That was a trick question. You don't give your partner attitude. You show her your attitude by playing the ♠A. You have six spades, dummy has three spades and partner has shown up with at least one spade, which means declarer has at most three spades. You control the spade suit. If declarer does have three spades, partner has a singleton king and no way to get to you to cash the other two spade tricks. Overtake partner's ♠K with your ♠A and then lead the ♠Q.

If both declarer and partner follow, you can lead spades again and maybe partner can overruff, or maybe it promotes a trump trick for her. If partner shows out on the second spade, you get to win a third spade trick. Your partner will discard on the second and third spade tricks and through these discards provide you information on what suit she would prefer you to lead next.

In situations like this one, the best way to show your attitude is to take charge — it's the clearest way to let your partner know the scoop.

## COROLLARY TO DEFENSE DISCIPLINE #4:
### On partner's first lead, give attitude; on subsequent leads, give count. On opponent's lead, give count.

Standard count is high-low to indicate an even number of cards and low-high to signify an odd number of cards. You should be aware that, just like for attitude, some partnerships use upside-down count, which reverses those meanings. We'll keep it simple in this book and utilize standard count. You should always look at your opponents' convention card to make sure what approach they are using. Never assume; always check.

Let's practice a few count signals. We'll assume the opponents are in a 3NT contract. West (your partner) opened proceedings with a low heart, you played high and declarer (South) played higher. Declarer then led the ♠4. Here are dummy's (North's) remaining twelve cards:

$$
\begin{array}{ll}
\spadesuit & K\,Q\,J\,10\,3 \\
\heartsuit & 8\,7 \\
\diamondsuit & 10\,9 \\
\clubsuit & 8\,6\,3
\end{array}
$$

Now before we worry about your cards, what do we know from South's spade play? Unless he's playing some mind game with you, he does not have the ♠A. If he had the ♠A, he would normally lead it first, win the second spade trick in dummy with the ♠K and run the spades, forcing you to discard like crazy.

What else do you know? Dummy doesn't appear to have any entries outside spades.

Defensively, East-West must determine the right time to take their ♠A (assuming they can choose). When is the right time? East-West should hold off until the trick on which South plays his last spade. If East-West take the trick earlier, South still has a spade to lead to the dummy and all those good spades. If East-West take it later, they have allowed declarer to win more spade tricks than he is entitled to. While generosity is often a virtue, the bridge table is not a good place to express it by giving your opponents undeserved tricks.

How do you know how many spades South has? You don't, but whichever of East-West does not have the ♠A must give count to his partner so that the ♠A can be played on the right trick.

Using standard count and the holdings below, which card should West play after South leads the ♠4?

1) ♠ 9 7               2) ♠ 9 7 2          3) ♠ 9 7 5 2

1) Play the ♠9, the higher of your two spots, signifying an even number.
2) Play the ♠2, your lowest spade, signifying an odd number.
3) Play the ♠7. When you have four, signal using the second-highest card.

Now, let's shift to East's perspective. South leads the ♠4 and West plays the ♠2. Remember dummy (North) holds ♠ KQJ103. How should East play with each of these holdings?

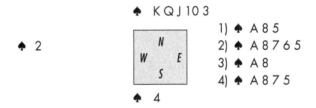

```
              ♠ K Q J 10 3
                              1) ♠ A 8 5
   ♠ 2          ┌───────┐     2) ♠ A 8 7 6 5
                │   N   │     3) ♠ A 8
                │ W   E │     4) ♠ A 8 7 5
                │   S   │
                └───────┘
              ♠ 4
```

1) East knows his partner has an odd number of spades since she played the lowest possible spade. There are five spades missing, including the one declarer led, so partner has either one or three spades. If West has three spades, then South started with a doubleton; East should duck the first trick and take the second round of spades, cutting South off from the rest of dummy's good spade tricks. If West has a singleton ♠2, it means South started out with four. Would North-South end up in a notrump contract with a nine-card spade fit? Unlikely, but possible — and if so, it doesn't matter when East plays his ♠A since South will have more than enough entries to score four spade tricks.

East should therefore hold off on the first spade trick and take the second. He shouldn't worry about the case where South does have four spades because his play makes no difference, and it's likely North-South are in the wrong contract!

2) Between East's cards and dummy's, he can account for ten spades. South's lead and West's ♠2 account for two more, leaving only one unaccounted for. West (with an odd number) must have a singleton and South a doubleton. Hold up on the first spade trick and take the second. West will be out of spades on the second trick and will be able to signal to help you decide which suit to lead next.

3) Technically, West could have one, three or five spades and South have the opposite — five, three or one. It's hard to believe North-South would miss a ten-card spade fit. If South has three spades it doesn't matter when you play your ace because South will still have entries to dummy. It is also unlikely that West has five and South a singleton — although it is possible. In any case, East might as well take the first trick just in case South has a singleton. There is no reason to give South an extra trick.

4) This time East has four spades; West again has three or one, leaving declarer with a singleton or three. How likely is it that South bid notrump with a singleton spade? Not very. On the other hand, if South has three then North-South have missed an eight-card fit. If East takes the first trick and it turns out partner has a singleton, North-South score two undeserved spade tricks. Similarly, if East delays taking the trick until the third round of spades and South does have a singleton, North-South again score two undeserved tricks. One advantage to the second approach is if West does have a singleton he can signal on the second spade trick, suggesting which suit to lead once East takes his spade trick.

To decide which choice to make you need to consider the bidding, any tricks already played and your knowledge of your opponents. Just because your partner signaled correctly doesn't mean you end up with a perfect picture of the opponent's holding.

In the next examples, West plays the ♠9 and everything else remains unchanged — the contract is 3NT.

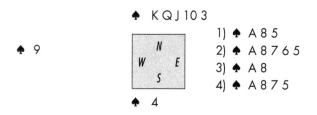

```
              ♠ K Q J 10 3
                                 1) ♠ A 8 5
   ♠ 9          ┌──────┐         2) ♠ A 8 7 6 5
                │   N  │         3) ♠ A 8
                │ W   E│         4) ♠ A 8 7 5
                │   S  │
                └──────┘
              ♠ 4
```

1) West has either a singleton ♠9 or a doubleton. If West has a singleton, South has four, North-South have missed a nine-card spade fit, and East can't stop them from collecting their spade tricks. Assume West has a doubleton, leaving South three. East needs to hold off until the third round.

2) Again spades split 2-1 between West and South. Taking the first trick gives North-South three undeserved tricks if South has a doubleton, which might be expected from his notrump bid. Taking the second trick only allows North-South one undeserved trick should South have the singleton. East should hold off until the second trick.

3) Probably West has two spot cards, and South has four — they missed a nine-card spade fit — unless West forgot that with four spots he should play the ♠7, or he suffered a mechanical error and pulled the wrong card. It does no harm to hold off until the second trick just in case West does have four spades and South only two. If West did make a mental or mechanical error, he'll be ever so grateful that his partner had his back.

4) In this situation it is again unclear whether West has a singleton or doubleton. A singleton leaves South with three, a doubleton leaves South with only two. To decide whether to hold off one or two rounds you need to consider what happens if you are wrong. If South has two spot cards and you hold off until the third round, you have given North-South one trick they did not deserve. If South has three spot cards and you take the second round, you give North-South two extra tricks.

   The first question to ask is whether either choice automatically allows North-South to make their contract. The main defensive objective is to defeat the contract. If it is a pure guess, and if North-South only need two spade tricks to make their contract, East should take the second trick. Giving the opponents two extra tricks is not something to brag about after the game, but allowing the opponents to make a contract they should not have made is much worse.

As we can see from these examples, giving accurate count when the opponents are on lead does not guarantee to provide partner all the information she needs to make a perfect contract-killing decision. However, in some cases it can be crucial.

When declarer is drawing trumps, your partner will rarely be making a hold-up play. However, there are times when partner needs to know if you have any trumps left to ruff one of declarer's good tricks. If you won't have an opportunity for a possible ruff and declarer is drawing them, you should play your trumps up the line starting with your lowest.

If you have the possibility of a ruff, then you give partner a high-low signal — called a **trump echo**. For example, with three trumps and the opportunity to get a ruff, you play your middle trump first, then your lowest. With luck, you will get to ruff with your highest trump. You can also perform a trump echo with four trumps if you want to tell partner that you expect to have trumps available and a suit in which you can use them for ruffs.

Here's an example to show how this standard understanding works. The opponents are in a 4♡ contract after the following bidding:

| West | North | East | South |
|------|-------|------|-------|
|      | 1NT   | pass | 2◇¹   |
| pass | 2♡²   | pass | 3NT   |
| pass | 4♡    | all pass |    |

1. Transfer to hearts.
2. Follows orders.

As West, with the ugly collection of cards shown below, you figure your only hope of helping partner defeat the contract might be to score a ruff in diamonds if your partner either has the ◇A or can take the first or second round of hearts and play a diamond back. You lead your singleton diamond and dummy comes down.

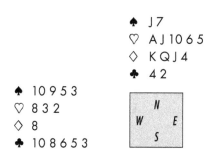

```
            ♠ J 7
            ♡ A J 10 6 5
            ◇ K Q J 4
            ♣ 4 2
♠ 10 9 5 3         N
♡ 8 3 2         W     E
◇ 8                S
♣ 10 8 6 5 3
```

Unfortunately, your partner does not have the ◇A, South does, and he wins the trick with it. Declarer now cashes the ♡K and you play the ♡3. When declarer now leads a low heart, you'll play the ♡2. He inserts dummy's ♡J and your partner takes the trick with the ♡Q. You, of course, know that if partner leads back a diamond you still have a trump left to ruff the trick. Your partner knows too because you gave him a high-low in hearts. If you only had two hearts (or three but no possibility to ruff in), you would have played the ♡2 first and then the ♡3.

With this knowledge your partner knows for sure you have a third trump, and she will confidently lead a diamond back for you to score your last trump.

Remember the trump echo is not about giving your partner an exact count. The key message with a trump echo is that you have at least one trump remaining and hope to convert it into a trick with a ruff.

If your trump suit holding were QJ10, would you use a trump echo? You have a natural trump trick that the declarer cannot steal from you. Generally, when you have a natural trump trick with a holding like this, you would not employ a trump echo, since it is usually better to eliminate two of their trumps with your trump.

Keep in mind that all the partnership signals we have discussed are general rules. As you become more advanced in defensive signals, you will learn exceptions to the rules, including when it is not necessary to give count and how to **falsecard**. I recommend you practice giving count. Your more advanced partners will appreciate it, and over time it will become second nature to you.

## DEFENSE DISCIPLINE #6:
### Visualize necessity.

This detail should sound familiar since it was also Declarer Device #3. It works equally well for defenders as it does for declarer. In fact, we'll even use a deal we discussed in the chapter on darned good declarer play to reintroduce the concept.

You may recall the deal from Chapter 2 where South was playing a 5♣ contract and North (the dummy) had most of the clubs. This time you are sitting West and lead the ♠K. Dummy is displayed and you proceed to analyze the situation.

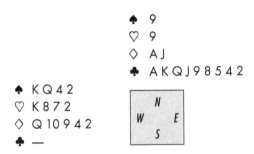

```
              ♠ 9
              ♡ 9
              ◇ A J
              ♣ A K Q J 9 8 5 4 2
  ♠ K Q 4 2
  ♡ K 8 7 2         N
  ◇ Q 10 9 4 2    W   E
  ♣ —               S
```

You count nine clubs on the board and quickly realize the only way to defeat this contract is if your partner has a trifecta of the ♠A, ♡A and the ◇K. Visualizing necessity, you place all three cards in your partner's hand and wait while declarer and partner catch up to your analysis.

The ♠K wins the trick (a very necessary step one) and, even if you miss the intent of partner's signal, you switch to a diamond. Declarer takes the trick in dummy with the ◇A and after finishing her fun with spades and clubs she has to lead either a heart or diamond. East can win both. Down one. Notice that you could have played a heart at Trick 2 to partner's ace, and let her switch to a diamond, but why give her the chance to go wrong? When you can make life easy for partner, do it!

Some logical thinking combined with visualizing necessity allows East-West to defeat this contract easily. As a defender, you can sometimes figure out the entire deal on your own. More often you will need help from your partner to score the maximum number of tricks.

## DEFENSE DISCIPLINE #7:
### Use suit preference to help your partner do the right thing.

Okay, I hear you saying, 'I'll give attitude on my partner's first lead of a suit. I've made a resolution to use count when it's appropriate. What happens when I don't have any of the suit led?' Unless you are ruffing the trick, you must make a discard, and since your partner already knows your attitude and count for that suit (you have none) you can signal your suit preference.

At most, you get to make a first discard once on each deal, so it is critical to use this opportunity to your advantage. You will run into a variety of discarding schemes at the club and at tournaments, but we're not going to worry about them just now. The examples in the book will use standard attitude discards.

Similar to standard attitude signals when your partner is on lead, discarding a high card signals your partner to lead the suit of your discard. When you can make a high standard discard, this is a great choice. It is usually quite clear and partner gets the message. It can also be dramatic. Let's say you are playing in a suit contract with hearts as trump. Dummy has two spades, extra hearts to make ruffs and your holding is ♠AKQx. Discard the ♠A. I guarantee (well, almost guarantee) partner will notice and lead a spade if she gets on lead.

Of course, sometimes you cannot afford to discard a high card to show your preference. In that situation, you must discard a low card from a suit you prefer not be led. Partner then must consider dummy, recall the bidding and the prior card play and determine which of the other two suits you want led. Usually this is not difficult for partner to figure out. However, sometimes none of your available discards can give partner the picture you want. That's bridge.

Let's look at an example where your suit preference signal provides partner a flashing neon sign advertising which suit you would like her to lead. This time you are sitting East, neither side vulnerable, and North-South bid to game in the following auction:

| West | North | East | South |
|------|-------|------|-------|
|      |       |      | 1♡ |
| 1♠ | 4♡ | all pass | |

You watch as partner leads the ♠A — the 'death card' of folklore fame — and you hope it's a good omen for defeating the opponents' contract. Bringing yourself back to the present, you study the dummy and make your plan.

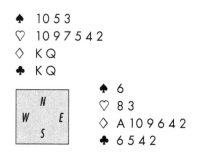

♠ 10 5 3
♡ 10 9 7 5 4 2
♦ K Q
♣ K Q

♠ 6
♡ 8 3
♦ A 10 9 6 4 2
♣ 6 5 4 2

The only trick you are likely to take is the ◊A. Your only concern is whether declarer can make dummy's diamonds disappear before you have a chance to take your trick. You need to tell partner that you want her to lead diamonds after she finishes taking her top spades. Who knows, maybe partner has a singleton and you can give her a ruff. Wouldn't that be nice?

On the first trick you play your spade. On the second trick partner leads the ♠J, which you take to mean he also has the ♠KQ. As long as partner didn't start with more than six spades, declarer will have at least three and partner will score three spade tricks. With the four top honors in the spade suit, partner may not have anything else. Declarer could easily have ♣AJxx and be able to pitch the two diamonds if he gets the chance.

Now is the time to shine with your suit-preference signal. You want partner to shift to a diamond after taking as many spade tricks as possible. (As soon as you show out of spades, partner will know how many spades declarer has and, therefore, whether or not three rounds will cash.)

Play your ◊10 to let partner know you would like a diamond return when the spades are done. Partner plays a third round of spades and then shifts to a diamond, leading the ◊8. You take your ◊A and declarer plays the ◊3. If partner had the ♣A, she probably would have cashed it for the setting trick, so you figure your only hope for another trick is if partner had a singleton diamond and you lead one back.

Declarer ruffs with the ♡A and claims, one down. Here's the complete deal:

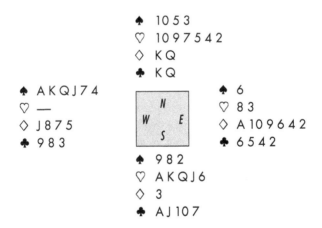

```
              ♠  10 5 3
              ♡  10 9 7 5 4 2
              ◊  K Q
              ♣  K Q
♠ A K Q J 7 4                    ♠  6
♡ —               N             ♡  8 3
◊ J 8 7 5    W         E        ◊  A 10 9 6 4 2
♣ 9 8 3           S             ♣  6 5 4 2
              ♠  9 8 2
              ♡  A K Q J 6
              ◊  3
              ♣  A J 10 7
```

Sure enough, if partner didn't switch to a diamond, declarer had four good clubs and would have brought the contract home. In this case your ◊10 was the 'death card' for their contract because it provided a treasure map for your partner to find your ace.

Another common opportunity for giving suit preference arises when you lead a suit you expect your partner will ruff. When you have more than one possible card to lead, your selection provides your partner information about how to get back to your hand so you can lead the original suit again and give your partner a second ruff.

Here's a deal that illustrates how this works. In an overly aggressive competitive auction with both sides vulnerable, your opponents reach a 4♠ contract. As East, you double. Your partner leads the ♣2 and dummy is tabled.

| West | North | East | South |
|------|-------|------|-------|
|      |       |      | pass  |
| 2♡   | pass  | 4♡   | 4♠    |
| pass | pass  | dbl  | all pass |

```
              ♠ J 7
              ♡ K 10
              ◇ K 7 6
              ♣ Q 9 8 7 5 3
Opening lead: ♣2         ♠ A 6 5
                  N      ♡ 8 6 5 3
               W     E   ◇ A 10
                  S      ♣ A J 10 4
```

Declarer promptly plays the ♣9 from dummy, and all eyes turn toward you. Ignoring the implied impatience, you plan your play. You need to decide whether to go up with the ♣A or, since the ♣Q is in dummy, insert the ♣10. How should you decide?

Your partner did not lead a heart. Why? Perhaps she has ♡AQ and did not want to lead away from the tenace and give declarer a cheap trick he didn't deserve.

How many clubs can declarer have? Dummy has six, you have four, partner just led one — only two are missing. Since partner led the lowest outstanding club, she either has ♣Kxx or a singleton. If partner's club is a singleton, then you want to go up with the ♣A and lead a club back to give her a ruff.

Combining dummy's two hearts, your four hearts and the six your partner should have for her bid leaves declarer with one heart. However, if declarer's singleton heart is the ♡A, the only reason for partner to lead a club instead of a heart is that the club is a singleton.

All that thinking only made the mud thicker. What else do you know about this hand? South came into the bidding late and at the four-level. To do that, his hand must be very distributional. Yet he didn't open 2♠, 3♠ or 4♠. He surely can't have more than five spades, so (a) they must be fairly decent (at least KQ109x or so) and (b) he must have a second suit, presumably diamonds. From partner's weak two, you know declarer has exactly one heart. So declarer either has five diamonds and two clubs, or (more likely) seven diamonds and no clubs. Why didn't he open 3◇? Well, his suit probably wasn't good enough, and with five decent spades as a side suit, it might not have seemed such a good idea to open 3◇ in front of partner. However, if he does have seven diamonds, that leaves partner with a singleton, and she didn't lead it.

Okay, back to the play at Trick 1. What if declarer is void in clubs? If you know that to be the case, you can save the ♣A to cover dummy's ♣Q and stick in the ♣10, since declarer will ruff it anyway. But your partner still has the ♣K even if your ♣A gets ruffed. Declarer will need to lead clubs from dummy twice before West's ♣K falls and then once more to score the ♣Q. There aren't enough entries in dummy to accomplish all those club leads. Whew! After all that thinking, you can play the ♣A to be on the safe side.

Declarer provides the ♣6. The only remaining club is the ♣K, which declarer must have (partner would not have led low from ♣Kx). With that added bit of information, you know that declarer is 5-1-5-2.

How many tricks can the defense take?

As soon as you lead a club back, partner will get her ruff and you will score your other two aces for down one (and if partner has the ♡A, down two). But wait — if partner by any chance has the ♡A, you can score another trick if you and partner cooperate.

If you can induce partner to lead back a diamond after she ruffs the club you are about to lead, you can win the ◇A and lead back your ◇10. Declarer must draw trumps before he can cash all his good diamonds. You can take the first spade trick with the ♠A, then you can lead a low heart to partner's hoped-for ♡A and she can lead a diamond back to you for your ruff.

Try hard not to salivate.

How can you tell partner to lead a diamond after she ruffs the club trick? Lead back your *lowest* club, the ♣4. (Partner already led the ♣2, and the ♣3 is in dummy, so there can be no question it is your lowest.) Your lowest club says, 'Partner, please return the lower of the remaining non-trump suits after you ruff this trick.'

Partner not only gets the hint but also holds the ♡A, and declarer does go down three. You score +800 points, a marvelous result, all because you and your partner communicated on defense.

Following is the whole deal:

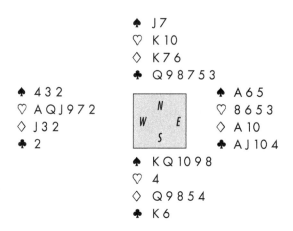

```
                        ♠ J 7
                        ♡ K 10
                        ◇ K 7 6
                        ♣ Q 9 8 7 5 3
    ♠ 4 3 2                               ♠ A 6 5
    ♡ A Q J 9 7 2          N              ♡ 8 6 5 3
    ◇ J 3 2          W          E         ◇ A 10
    ♣ 2                    S              ♣ A J 10 4
                        ♠ K Q 10 9 8
                        ♡ 4
                        ◇ Q 9 8 5 4
                        ♣ K 6
```

As you can see South did indeed have 5-1-5-2 shape, and his silly bid got what it deserved. Your deductions were correct and your partnership found all the right leads.

Twelve tables played this contract and only one reached the doubled 4♠ contract we just discussed. (I was actually sitting East and we played a 3♡ contract. Most of the other tables were in 4♡.) The East-West pair who defended just as I described got a great result for the deal. It may have been lucky for them that their opponents were the only ones to bid 4♠, but they still did a good job finding all the right plays including the suit-preference signal.

So far we have had your partner make the all-important first lead. Lean in close while I tell you about my hands down, all-time favorite opening lead — keep it a secret now. *The best lead from my standpoint is one someone else has to make!* Opening leads can be one of the most frustrating parts of the game. Sometimes it doesn't matter what you lead and, for all your thinking, you could randomly choose any card from your hand. Sometimes you find the perfect lead and set their contract. More often, the wrong lead provides the opposition with an extra trick they don't deserve.

As we discuss leads, be aware that given the same bidding sequence and the same thirteen cards in their hands, experts often choose different leads. There are few 'right' answers in leading, which doesn't mean you can just pick any card you choose. Your lead should be considered carefully. That's the best you can do; the rest depends on the lay of the cards.

To choose the right suit to lead you should reflect on the auction. What suit(s) did the opponents bid? What suit(s) did partner bid? What suit(s) did no one bid? Did the opponents boldly bid to their contract, or did they wander around the desert for forty days and forty nights before limping into game? Did they stop in a partscore?

Against notrump contracts, unless you have an honor sequence (like KQJ for example), you will often choose to lead your longest suit with the hope that you can set up future tricks in that suit. Having chosen the suit, now you have to choose which card to lead. My advice is to use standard leads because over time those have been found to be the most effective (or perhaps least ineffective). The standard length lead in notrump contracts is the fourth highest of your suit.

Why the fourth highest, and not the lowest or something in the middle? You hope to find partner with an honor in the suit you lead, which will make your holding much more valuable. Leading the fourth highest card allows your partner to use the Rule of Eleven to help determine how to play the suit. We discussed the Rule of Eleven in the previous chapter, but in case you have forgotten or are skipping around, here's how it works: if the lead is the fourth highest in a suit, the number of cards the other three players have that can beat that card equals eleven less the spot of the card led.

It is the ace's fault that the Rule of Eleven works. He didn't want to be a lowly one in the game of bridge; he wanted to be more important than the king. With thirteen cards in a suit we start counting with the two and proceed up to the ace. The jack becomes eleven the queen is twelve, the king is thirteen and the mighty ace is fourteen. When you lead fourth best, you hold three higher cards. The Rule of Eleven tells how many cards the other three hands hold.

If your fourth-best card is the jack (the eleven), you hold the ace, king and queen (forget for the moment that you wouldn't lead the jack from this holding!). No one else has a higher card, which is what the rule says ($11 - 11 = 0$). If your fourth highest card is the ten, you have three of the AKQJ and someone else has one of them ($11 - 10 = 1$). This works all the way down to the deuce: when you lead it, you still have three higher cards and everyone else has nine of them ($11 - 2 = 9$).

Both declarer and the leader's partner can see how many cards dummy has in that suit that can beat the lead. They each know how many cards in their hand beat the lead, which means declarer can determine how many cards the leader's partner has that beat the opening lead, and the leader's partner can determine the same for declarer.

Wait! Doesn't this mean you are giving away valuable information to declarer when you make a fourth-highest lead? Yes, but when you choose that suit you hope your side can get the majority of the tricks in that suit, and to accomplish that it is more important for your partner to understand how the suit lies than to hide the information from declarer. That's why it is so important for both defenders to be on the same wavelength.

Previously, we discussed the idea of leading bottom from three small against a suit contract, so as to avoid having partner think you have a doubleton. But from three small in notrump contracts the standard lead is the top card. This indicates to partner that the suit is not where you have length. So if you see a small card lead from partner, you will assume it is from length. With a higher spot card, you will presume it is not a length lead. If partner leads a middle spot card, you need to look at your spots and dummy's and usually you can figure out if it is a length lead or from the top of nothing.

Let's look at an example from a deal in which you sit East. South opened 1NT and they ended up in 3NT.

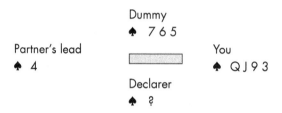

Dummy
♠ 7 6 5

Partner's lead
♠ 4

You
♠ Q J 9 3

Declarer
♠ ?

West leads the ♠4 against 3NT, dummy comes down and you apply the Rule of Eleven to try to determine who has what. There are seven cards higher than the ♠4 in North's, South's and East's combined hands. North has three, you have three; therefore South must have only one. Since you have the ♠3 and declarer opened 1NT, you begin with the assumption that South started with two cards: the ♠2 and something higher.

After you play your ♠J, South takes the trick with his ♠K. Now you figure South had ♠K2 and partner started with the ♠A1084 — unless declarer is one of those folks who open 1NT with a singleton king, in which case partner started off with five spades, not the four you originally assumed. When you win a trick in another suit, you can lead back the ♠Q, at which point you and partner will both find out exactly what South's holding was.

Because partner led a low spade, you knew it was from length and could figure out the spade holdings.

In a later hand in the same match, partner leads the ♡8 after the opponents bid 1NT - 3NT.

Dummy
♡ 7 6 5

Partner's lead
♡ 8

You
♡ Q J 9 3

Declarer
♡ ?

This looks like a top of nothing lead and partner is fishing in the majors trying to set up your suit. It's just possible that partner started out with ♡AK108, since the Rule of 11 tells you that if it was a length lead, there are three unaccounted-for cards between the opponents and you, and you have them all. Unless you've been winning a lot of lottery tickets recently, you had best initially plan that declarer has the missing honors. In any event, play your ♡J and the heart suit will be crystal clear once declarer plays.

When declarer wins with the ace, you know he has your heart holding under the gun. The only way you will score a trick is if declarer only has three hearts and you are able to lead the thirteenth heart.

The standard leads are time-tested. The last two examples illustrate how using standard leads can help the defense stay the course of the initial lead or determine that a shift in suits is necessary. Advanced players may play a different system of leads, but with most partners, utilizing standard leads will work well.

When your partner makes an opening lead, spend some time thinking about your defensive options based on her lead. I found the Eddie Kantar software on bridge defense to be a great help to me in understanding standard defensive carding and leads.

## DEFENSE DISCIPLINE #8:
### Pick the right suit to lead.

Before you can decide which card to lead, you have to choose which suit to lead. I wish I could share some infallible rules, but there are none. You can find deals here and there in which some off-the-wall lead sets a contract no normal lead could have. Here are some suggestions that will help you win more consistently:

### 1) If your partner bid — lead her suit.
One of my recent partners sports a tee shirt that lists three reasons for not leading your partner's suit: (1) You have a void. (2) You forgot the bidding. (3) You want a new partner. It may not work out, but it is much easier to lead your partner's suit, whether or not it succeeds, than to explain to partner why you didn't lead her suit and let the opponents make the contract.

However, if you have the ace in her suit without the king, despite the tee shirt's short list of excuses, you should consider whether leading the suit is likely to cost a trick. For example, if your partner overcalls 1♠ and the opponents end up in 3♡, with a hand like

♠J7  ♡K10  ◊K76  ♣Q98753

lead the ♠J.

However, if we change your hand to

♠A75  ♡106  ◊76  ♣KQJ753

a club lead looks attractive. Won't your partner be upset that you didn't lead her suit? No, she'll know you have a very good reason. Maybe (as with this hand) you have a better natural lead and she'll learn from your lead how to defeat the contract.

If that's not the case, she will assume you have the ace in her suit and play the cards accordingly, perhaps trapping the declarer's king or queen.

This is the kind of position that comes up all the time in suit contracts.

Dummy
♠ 10 7

You
♠ A 3 2

Partner
♠ Q J 9 6 5

Declarer
♠ K 8 4

If you lead any spade it sets up declarer's king. However, if any other player breaks the spade suit (i.e. is the first to lead it), your side can capture all the available spade tricks.

Of course with a layout of

Dummy
♡ Q 7 4

You
♡ A 3 2

Partner
♡ K J 10 6 5

Declarer
♡ 9 8

leading the ace finds partner sitting behind dummy's queen. Unless declarer can immediately score all his needed tricks, you are still going to get all of your heart tricks once either you or partner regains the lead.

So in suit contracts, if you have a good lead in another suit (like a sequence or a singleton) try that. Your partner will gather you have the ace in her suit (or maybe figure you for a void). If you decide to lead partner's suit, then plunk down the ace.

In a notrump contract, your best lead may well be your partner's suit. If you have the ace doubleton, you must lead the ace to unblock the suit for partner. With ace and two small cards, you can afford to lead small and unblock on the second lead of the suit. With ace and three or more small, you'll make the standard fourth best lead.

### 2) Don't underlead aces against suit contracts.

I know, sometimes it works. More frequently, as in the spade example above, it does not succeed and the opponents score a king or queen your ace should have taken. Remember, the opponents won the auction, so unless they are sacrificing, they have the majority of the points. Especially if this isn't a suit your partner bid, it is much more likely for them to have the king and/or queen in the suit than your partner.

There is another reason not to lead away from your ace in suit contracts. Sometimes dummy or declarer has a singleton in the suit and you end up never scoring your ace. If you had led something else, you would have seen dummy's singleton and known how to play the suit when it was led. You won't see a singleton in declarer's hand, but by the time the suit is played you may know enough to deduce declarer's shortness in the suit.

In notrump contracts you often lead away from an ace if it is in the long suit you are trying to set up. As you know, the standard lead in that situation is your fourth highest in the suit.

### 3) Don't lead an ace in an unbid suit (unless you have the king too).

Some I/Ns learn too well the lesson not to lead away from their aces. Instead, they immediately plunk down an ace to avoid losing it. They're worried that declarer will manage to get rid of his losers in that suit before they can score the ace. Yes, it's true; sometimes you'll go to bed with your ace because you didn't lead it at Trick 1. But aces are best used for taking kings and queens. Unless partner has bid the suit, leading an ace gives you a much better chance of gathering a 'wish trick' (A-2-3-4) than one loaded with your opponents' honors.

However, if you have the ace and king, then leading the ace (or king, depending on your partnership agreement) is usually an excellent lead. You and your partner get to see dummy. Your partner gets to signal her attitude toward the suit you led, and unless declarer or dummy has a void, you retain the lead.

### 4) Lead from an honor sequence if you have one.

If you have a sequence (for example QJ10) or even a broken sequence (QJ9), thank your lucky stars you drew a hand with a natural lead. In a suit contract, two connected honors suffice; in a notrump contract, you should have three in the sequence before leading it.

The advantages of leading from a sequence headed by the ace-king are obvious: you win the trick (unless someone has a void), you and partner get to see dummy (so does declarer, of course), and partner can signal whether or not she is interested in the suit.

Leading other sequences provides many of the same benefits. Although you may not retain the lead, you do get to find out your partner's attitude toward the suit and the lead is unlikely to cost a trick. When leading from an unbroken sequence, it is standard to lead the top card (for example king from KQx in a trump contract or from KQ10x in a notrump contract). When leading a broken sequence (like KJ10 in a suit contract or AJ109 in a notrump contract) you should choose the top card after the break (the jack in each case here).

This next position illustrates the difference in honor leads between suit and notrump contracts:

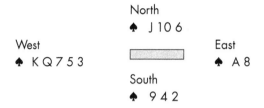

North
♠ J 10 6

West
♠ K Q 7 5 3

East
♠ A 8

South
♠ 9 4 2

Against a suit contract, West leads the ♠K. East can overtake with the ♠A, lead the ♠8 back to West's ♠Q and get a ruff. Alternately, if the bidding or cards in the other suit dictate otherwise, East can choose to play the ♠8 on the first trick, which blocks the suit. If North-South have no place to stick the losing spade trick, blocking the suit may not matter as West can always score the ♠Q later. Either way, the defense can get three tricks.

In a notrump contract East has a problem if West leads the ♠K. If he overtakes with the ♠A and leads back the ♠8, West can only set up the suit after giving declarer a spade trick. The standard lead of fourth highest by West (the ♠5) avoids this problem. East takes the first trick with the ♠A and leads back the ♠8, which West takes with the ♠Q. West then proceeds to run off the remaining spade tricks after playing the ♠K, dropping North's ♠J. Five tricks off the top, and unless declarer has all the remaining tricks, he can't even make 2NT.

### 5) Lead a singleton against suit contracts.

On many deals, leading a singleton is the ticket to success. It works perfectly when your partner can win with the ace and lead the suit back so you can score a ruff. Even if your partner cannot take the first trick, you may still score a ruff if either of you can win an early trump trick.

Should you always lead a singleton? Of course not. If your opponents bid the suit, it is less likely your partner has the ace, diminishing your chances of an immediate ruff. Also, leading a singleton in their bid suit increases the likelihood you are leading through partner's honor and giving declarer an easy way to bring in the suit. Leading a singleton honor comes with added risks. If you lead a singleton jack or queen, you may have solved declarer's finessing problems.

Also, if the trump you plan to use for the ruff is a natural trump trick (for example you hold QJ10) it is usually better to force declarer to draw trumps (reducing his own ability to ruff) rather than try for a ruff yourself.

A good time to lead a singleton is when you have an early trump stopper. That way if your partner is not so accommodating as to have the ace in your singleton suit, when declarer leads trumps you can capture the lead. Then, with the added information you've gained from seeing dummy, you can (with luck) find a way into your partner's hand so she can lead back your original suit and give you the ruff.

## 6) Don't lead a singleton in an unbid suit against notrump contracts.

The classic (mistaken) case for wanting to lead a singleton occurs when the bidding goes 1NT — 3NT. Dummy won't have four of a major (unless his hand is perfectly flat, then he might), so the thinking goes something along the lines of: if I only have one heart (or spade), then partner should have five, maybe even six. If I lead my singleton, I'll help partner set up her long suit.

It sounds logical, and might even work on occasion, but it has a dark side that more often than not prevails. When you break a suit, it means the opponents don't have to, and it often costs a trick or two in the suit. Declarer may have a two-way finesse that you clarify for him with your lead in a position such as:

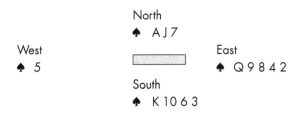

North
♠ A J 7

West
♠ 5

East
♠ Q 9 8 4 2

South
♠ K 10 6 3

Or perhaps there is a natural way for declarer to play the cards, but you've given him a free peek as here:

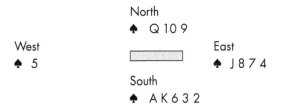

North
♠ Q 10 9

West
♠ 5

East
♠ J 8 7 4

South
♠ A K 6 3 2

Left to play the suit himself, South would very likely cash two top honors. Your lead allows him to get five winners in spades; his natural play would mean his losing one trick.

## 7) Rarely lead a doubleton against suit contracts.

This suggestion applies when partner has not bid the suit. Leading a singleton in order to score a ruff works if your partner has the ace or can take a quick trump trick and lead back the suit before you run out of trumps. To score a ruff from a doubleton holding, you need three leads of the suit before you run out of trumps. In partner's bid suit the chances for a ruff improve, but often you need an early trump trick in your hand (Ax or Kxx sitting behind the ace) and a way to your partner's hand in order to score a ruff when you have a doubleton.

Particularly avoid leading doubleton honors. Sure you can luck out with a Kx holding — find your partner with Axx, and by leading the king score the first two tricks and a ruff when your partner leads the third round. However, unless the bidding tells you otherwise, the opponents are twice as likely to have the ace as your partner. Half of those times your king is sitting behind their ace, and if you didn't lead the suit you would score the king. By leading it you only succeed in giving your opponents an extra trick.

In this next example we'll help West consider what to lead against a 4♠ contract arrived at with this bidding:

| West | North | East | South |
|------|-------|------|-------|
|  | 1◇ | pass | 1♠ |
| pass | 1NT | pass | 2♣[1] |
| pass | 2♠ | pass | 4♠ |
| all pass |  |  |  |

1. New Minor Forcing, implying five spades and an invitational or better hand.

West's hand is

♠A75  ♡86  ◇9765  ♣Q853

What does the bidding tell us? North (dummy) has a minimum opening count, probably four or more diamonds and exactly three spades since he only supported South's spade bid after the 2♣ New Minor Forcing bid. North-South have game points, but not enough for slam. You have only 6 HCP. Partner (East) must have a few points unless the opponents missed slam. She could have as many as 9 HCP, but probably has fewer. She had the chance to bid hearts at the one level and did not, so you know she doesn't have five or more decent hearts and enough points to overcall.

Let's consider each suit to determine which we might want to lead. Spades is their trump suit. If dummy's main value is to ruff declarer's losers, it might be good to try to remove two spades from dummy by leading the ♠A and continuing with another spade. But North showed flattish distribution with his bidding, so a spade lead isn't jumping up and down and saying, 'I'm definitely the one'.

Harry Truman wanted to meet a one-armed economist because all of his kept saying, 'on the other hand…' Talking about bridge leads has the same characteristic — there is often another side to consider. Although dummy has flattish distribution, it could certainly include a doubleton and then taking two spades off the board could be the right thing.

If you lead your doubleton heart you need the right cards in partner's hand to get your ruff. You are well positioned in spades to secure a ruff because with the ace and two small you will regain the lead while you still have trumps remaining. To score your ruff, you'll need partner to have first- or second-round control of hearts and possibly an entry to get back to her hand. Obviously if she has ♡AKxx, you've got your ruff. Even if partner has ♡Axx you can still get your ruff. On the opening lead, partner will duck (if she can figure you for a doubleton — another reason for standard leads!). Declarer will win the trick, but as soon as declarer tries to draw trumps you will pop up with your ace and lead your second heart. Partner will win the ace and lead a third heart for you to ruff.

If partner doesn't have the ace, your ruff becomes much less likely. For example, if partner has ♡KQx, declarer can hold up his ace on the first trick and take the second. Once you regain the lead with your trump ace, you must find another immediate entry into partner's hand — a doubtful proposition. Even with your sure early trump trick, you need your rose-tinted glasses to envision a heart ruff coming your way.

You have no diamond values and North opened the bidding with them. North probably does not have six diamonds since he didn't rebid them, but he could have five. Choosing a diamond might 'lead through strength' (see #8 below for more on that topic) but it also might serve to help declarer set up the suit. Without more information, I'd reject a diamond, unless, of course, other leads are even less attractive.

You have a club honor and no one has bid the suit. Even if partner has good clubs, she probably does not have enough points to overcall at the two-level. All it would take is for partner to have something like the ♣KJx for clubs to be a good lead, setting up two possible club winners before they could be pitched off on (say) good diamonds. Of course, leading from such a moth-eaten suit could just as easily set up a trick for declarer.

Before finishing your analysis, you need to think a bit about where four tricks to defeat the contract might come from. Unless you revoke, your ♠A is guaranteed, leaving three more. Even if you score a couple of clubs, you are still one short. The best hope looks like partner having the ♡A so you can score a ruff. That will make three tricks, and between your ♣Q and the other points you expect partner to have (maybe a king of clubs or diamonds?), with luck you can eke out a fourth trick.

You have no perfect lead, but odds appear to favor a heart lead to take the first step toward developing four defensive tricks.

## 8) Lead through strength, not into it.

As declarer you like nothing better than a lead that sets up a trick in your hand. If you have the AQ and your LHO leads the suit, it guarantees you'll score both tricks (assuming no ruffs). Declarers also get a warm tingly feeling when their LHO leads a suit in which they hold the Kx. Declarer can score the king on the first trick if the ace does not appear, or if it does, his king is now top dog. If you lead a suit that declarer bid, you stand a good chance of giving him an extra trick.

On the other hand, declarers are not fond of making decisions earlier than they have to. If you are not worried about setting up a long suit in dummy that declarer can eventually run, sometimes leading through dummy's strength can force declarer to make guesses before he has additional information to help him. For example, if dummy has AQ10 and declarer has xxx in the suit you led, declarer has no feel for where the defenders' points are located (unless they have bid) and may guess wrong about how to play the suit.

### 9) Lead trumps (except when you shouldn't).

Sometimes a trump lead is a good one; sometimes it's neutral; and sometimes it's atrocious. Maybe you've heard the adage, 'When in doubt, lead trumps'. Don't believe it. Someone trying to justify a terrible trump lead pawned that statement off on a gullible partner. Rely on the bidding and your hand to help you decide whether leading trumps is a good idea or not.

One indicator is when dummy's bidding indicates trump support but not too many points. In such a situation, the main value of dummy's hand is often its ability to ruff your winners. For example, consider this auction with North-South vulnerable:

| West | North | East | South |
|------|-------|------|-------|
|      |       |      | 1◇ |
| pass | 1♡ | pass | 2♣ |
| all pass |    |      |       |

This bidding strongly suggests leading trumps could be just the ticket. North has shown a preference for South's second suit. Yes, North did not bid clubs, but the fact he did not correct to diamonds with a 2◇ bid shows that he prefers clubs and does not believe they have enough points for game. Often in this bidding sequence you'll find dummy short in the first bid suit (diamonds).

For example, you might hold:

♠ 10 8 5 3   ♡ Q 5   ◇ K 7 5 4   ♣ Q 8 2

You have 7 HCP. Your partner must have a number of HCP. You and your partner have both read the first chapter on bidding and learned the value of competing, but she didn't reopen the bidding even though the opponents stopped at the two-level.

Leading clubs immediately eliminates one of dummy's trumps. If the deal looks something like this, your opening trump lead saves a trick:

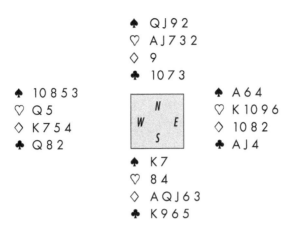

```
                    ♠ Q J 9 2
                    ♡ A J 7 3 2
                    ◇ 9
                    ♣ 10 7 3
    ♠ 10 8 5 3                         ♠ A 6 4
    ♡ Q 5          ┌─────────┐         ♡ K 10 9 6
    ◇ K 7 5 4      │    N    │         ◇ 10 8 2
    ♣ Q 8 2        │ W     E │         ♣ A J 4
                   │    S    │
                   └─────────┘
                    ♠ K 7
                    ♡ 8 4
                    ◇ A Q J 6 3
                    ♣ K 9 6 5
```

If you lead a low club, with careful play you can hold North-South to eight tricks. In this deal, leading a heart (would you really have done that? — not I) also holds the contract to eight tricks. Leading a spade (the unbid suit) or a diamond gives them an extra trick.

Let's say you lead the ♣2, your partner looks at dummy, sees the singleton diamond and decides you had a good idea. She takes her ♣A and leads another club, which South takes. South leads the ◇A and then the ◇Q. Do you cover with the ◇K or not?

If South didn't have the ◇J, he would have led a low diamond to get the ruff in dummy. Given he led the ◇Q, I'd also place the ◇J in his hand. He doesn't know where the ◇K is, and I don't see any reason to let him off the hook. I expect he will let the queen ride, but who knows? He might get nervous and ruff his good trick. Stranger things have happened and, as in declarer play, as a defender I like to allow my opponents the opportunity to make mistakes. So I'd duck the ◇Q. If South lets it ride (which he does), I'll cover whatever diamond he leads next.

After that fun, South can win two spade tricks, a heart trick and one club for a total of eight tricks.

What happens if West leads spades, the unbid suit? East dutifully hops up with the ♠A. It doesn't matter what East tries at this point, East-West can only take three more tricks. Why? East can still eliminate two of dummy's trumps by leading the ♣A and then another club. The problem is that by leading spades, you set up three spade tricks for declarer.

Leading trumps usually helps your cause when the opponents are sacrificing. In sacrifice situations your side has the majority of the points. Their only hope is to score as many trumps as possible by ruffing your good tricks. They would especially like to set up a crossruff.

Sometimes you are not sure whether the opponents are sacrificing. For example, on this deal with East-West vulnerable, the bidding is as follows:

| West | North | East | South |
|------|-------|------|-------|
| 1♠ | 2NT[1] | 4♠ | 5◇ |
| dbl | all pass | | |

1. Shows at least 5-5 in the minors.

Sitting West you hold

♠A Q 7 6 4   ♡A 8 6   ◇A 8 2   ♣K J

After your 1♠ bid you planned to show your extra points on your second bid, but never got the chance. Worse, it's up to you to lead.

Many things are not clear. You have a very nice hand, but the distribution is obviously wonky on this deal. North's bid shows both minors. He should have at least 5-5 distribution in the minors, although people do sometimes cheat and make the bid with only 5-4. Partner's jump to 4♠ probably shows a weak hand with five spades, which means the opponents' spades are at best split 2-1 with 3-0 not unlikely. South's 5◇ bid could be a sacrifice, or it could be a legitimate bid. You have three diamonds; partner is likely to have, at most, one of them. Partner did choose to leave the double in rather than pull it. If she had no defensive tricks, she might have pulled it, so you can hope partner has a few points.

With every expectation that partner has the ♠K, you could choose to lead the ♠A. But if she has five spades to the jack with points in the other suits, it would be a bummer to have the ace ruffed out and set up the ♠K for the opponents. Let's see what the other suits have to offer.

You have no clue who has the ♡K, so leading the ♡A is much less attractive than leading the ♠A. Not hearts.

Leading a club is a double-edged sword, mostly pointed at your throat. All partner needs is the ace or queen to make you look smart. However, given that North claims five clubs sitting behind you, a club lead could solve declarer's problems in a hurry. Besides, those tricks, if they exist, are unlikely to go away. A club looks too scary for me.

Well, this section is about trump leads, and that means considering diamonds. If South's 5◇ was a sacrifice based on ruffing power, leading a couple rounds of trumps will be just the thing. If it was a legitimate 5◇ bid, leading a diamond at least has the advantage of being less likely to give a trick away. With that thinking, in the past I might have led the ◇A in order to retain the lead, observe dummy and continue diamonds if it made sense or shift suits if a better opportunity was apparent. However, with a bit more experience I'd try a low diamond instead.

Why does a low diamond make sense? Well, first, I'd feel like a real dodo if my ace dropped partner's singleton king. 'Oops, sorry' doesn't quite cover that gaffe. Secondly, if declarer is going to set up a crossruff, I expect it to involve hearts or spades. He'll need to clear out the chosen suit and I have the aces to regain the lead in both majors. Even in clubs I have at worst third-round control (by trumping). If my partner is void in diamonds (a real possibility given the bidding), she has an opportunity to give me a suit-preference signal on the first trick regardless of whether or not I win that trick. If she has a singleton, then if I take the second diamond trick, she can give me a suit-preference signal on that trick. Either way, I'll have a good feel for my options when I regain the lead. And if I want to continue trumps, I'll be able to clear out three rounds of them.

Here are the four hands:

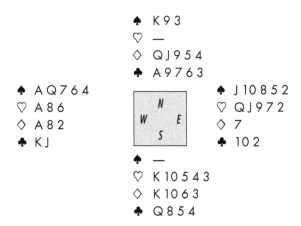

Sure enough, leading anything other than a trump costs East-West a trick, and North-South make their contract. Although I thought the reentry to my hand would likely be through hearts or spades, it turned out the opponents had voids in both those suits and it was the club king that allowed me to get in and pull trumps. My partner was wise to leave the double in, since East-West can only make ten tricks in spades.

Another good time to lead trumps is when you make a one-level takeout double and your partner passes:

| West | North | East | South |
|------|-------|------|-------|
|      |       |      | 1♡    |
| dbl  | pass  | pass | pass  |

Partner's pass means she thinks the best score you can receive on this deal is from defending the doubled 1♡ contract. She will only do this with a stack of hearts — probably including several honors — and she wants to draw declarer's trumps.

With a hand like

♠ A 10 7 6   ♡ 8   ◇ A K 8 2   ♣ K J 6 5

you should lead the ♡8 since you aren't going to ruff anything with it. South and your partner, East, have most of the hearts. You would hate for South to be able to ruff one of your good tricks. You might be tempted to lead the ◇A to get a feel for dummy. However, the trick is unlikely to disappear, and if dummy happens to have a singleton diamond and two trumps, you may have given declarer a chance for an undeserved ruff.

Although some bidding sequences call for opening trump leads, other situations should scream, 'No!' If your partner didn't double the contract, leading a singleton trump is usually a bad play. If you have only one, chances are your partner has three or four and leading a trump will perform a free finesse for the opponents. If you lead trumps when the opponents are in a misfit, you might finesse your partner in a situation where declarer has insufficient entries to dummy to do it for himself.

Similarly, if you yourself have four trumps your attitude changes from trying to eliminate ruffing opportunities for declarer to trying to wrest trump control from him. Lead your longest suit in hopes that he will need to ruff it. If you (and your partner) can make him ruff a few more times, you may snag trump control. At the least, it can help promote your trumps to winners. Take this same approach if you think partner has four trumps. Lead a suit you hope declarer will eventually need to ruff and maybe partner can take over trump control from declarer.

Holding

♠ Q 10 7 6 5　♡ J 6　◇ 8 7 6 2　♣ K 10

against a 3◇ contract in which you believe declarer has five diamonds and dummy has three, consider leading a spade. If declarer has to ruff once, you'll have the same number of trumps remaining as he does. If you and partner can force declarer to ruff again, you will now have more trumps than declarer.

Another time to avoid leading trumps is when the bidding indicates dummy has a long suit that you suspect declarer can run and dummy has also shown trump support. In that scenario the betting line is for declarer to clear trumps and then run dummy's long suit, pitching losers along the way. This situation calls for an attacking lead. Don't lead trumps; don't lead dummy's long suit. Choose whichever of the remaining two suits looks more likely to score some quick tricks and let 'er rip.

For example, holding

♠ Q 10 6 5　♡ 6 5　◇ 8 6 2　♣ K 10 9 3

with the following bidding, what would you lead?

| West | North | East | South |
|------|-------|------|-------|
|      | 1◊    | pass | 1♡    |
| pass | 3◊    | pass | 3NT   |
| pass | 4♡    | all pass |   |

From the bidding it is clear North has a passel of diamonds that are going to be crammed down your throat as soon as declarer clears trumps. North has also made it clear he has heart support because he pulled the 3NT contract to 4♡, where North-South have to collect an additional trick in order to make game.

On this kind of strong bidding you need to collect your tricks in a hurry. With any delay, declarer can set up the diamond tricks and your chances are burnt toast. All other things being equal, choose your strongest suit and lead that. In this hand, your clubs are stronger than your spades since they are headed by the king and have the ten and nine as intermediate values. As well, partner had a chance to overcall with a 1♠ bid and didn't, which also gives the nod to clubs.

Suppose your ♣K changed to an ace and you held

♠Q 10 6 5  ♡6 5  ◊8 6 2  ♣A 10 9 3

Because of the urgency to take your tricks very quickly, many experts would choose to lead the ♣A in hopes partner had the king. Remember your intent is to defeat the contract. You may very well give them an extra trick with the lead of your ace, but it still seems to offer you the best chance of success. If it doesn't work, it's not my fault! Pick up your next hand and carry on.

### 10) Make attacking leads against small slams in a suit.
A contract of six of a suit almost always calls for an attacking lead. If you lead passively you may give the opponents enough opportunity to use their trumps to set up a long side suit on which to pitch losers. You need to strike first so when they lose the one trick they expected to lose, you can immediately take the setting trick. You won't get another chance.

Lead low from a suit like K986, and if your partner has the ace you'll score two tricks right away (as long as neither opponent has a singleton or void). By leading low you also score your king if partner has the queen and either of you wins a trick in another suit. Remember, don't lead *away* from an ace. You might even choose to lead your ace and let your partner's signal guide you regarding what to lead to the second trick.

### 11) Listen to the bidding.
Although we have incorporated Defensive Discipline #5 (*draw inferences from the bidding*) in many of the examples, it is so important when you are considering your opening lead that it bears repeating. Often, if you close your eyes and replay the

bidding, the suit you should lead is obvious. Then open your eyes and choose the right card to lead from that suit. Sometimes the opponents dance around notrump before exhaustedly falling into a 3NT contract. They often have the points for the contract, but may have only one stopper in their weak suit.

After this bidding what suit should you lead?

| West | North | East | South |
|------|-------|------|-------|
| pass | 1♠ | pass | 1NT[1] |
| pass | 2♣ | pass | 3◇ |
| pass | 3♠ | pass | 3NT |
| all pass | | | |

1. Forcing.

Since you have not run up against this particular sequence involving the 3◇ bid, you ask North what you need to know and are told that it shows opening points and a good diamond suit.

North-South settled into a 3NT contract, and from the bidding you know South has diamonds and points. North probably has exactly five spades (didn't rebid them after the forcing 1NT) and does not have four hearts (bid clubs rather than hearts after the forcing 1NT). South presumably has a heart stopper, but if it isn't the ace, maybe you can capture his honor and run hearts before they get started on the other three suits.

Time to look at your hand

♠ 10 7 3   ♡ K 6 5   ◇ 7 4   ♣ J 9 8 5 2

and decide if you have a heart lead that makes sense. It's a notrump contract. You consider your long clubs. Length makes strength. North could make his club bid with only three clubs. Perhaps you should lead the ♣5 — fourth best of your longest and strongest — and use the ♡K as an entry back to the clubs. I/N's who always choose the 'fourth best' lead should remember the joke told by a frustrated player who, when asked about their partnership leads, lamented 'We lead fourth best — there are always three better leads!'

The listening exercise suggests hearts. Clubs might work well, but the suit they danced around was hearts. Could partner have good hearts and not have overcalled? She would have had to bid them at the two-level, and probably doesn't have enough points to do that. If you choose to lead hearts, which one should it be? From three to an honor, the standard lead is the low one.

Your other choice is to lead something passive and hope for the best. But North-South bid everything except hearts, and if South wins the first trick he might be able to run his diamonds and score at least nine tricks off the top.

For better or worse, I'd go with what my ears sensed at the beginning and lead the ♡5. Dummy appears and you see how good your analysis was.

```
              ♠ K Q J 9 2
              ♡ 7 3
              ◇ Q
              ♣ A Q 10 7 3
  ♠ 10 7 3          ┌─────────┐
  ♡ K 6 5           │    N    │
  ◇ 7 4             │ W     E │
  ♣ J 9 8 5 2       │    S    │
                    └─────────┘
```

You study dummy. What if South has diamonds that run? With the ♠A he gets nine or ten tricks off the top. What if diamonds don't run because partner has the ◇A? South probably has the ♠A and ♣K for his 3NT bid. If he has at least one more club to go with the ♣K, South can finesse against your ♣J and make five spades and four clubs for his nine tricks.

Maybe you are getting ahead of yourself. If South has the ♡A, the party is probably over anyhow. Declarer is finished analyzing the situation and plays the ♡3 from dummy. Partner provides the needed ♡A, and South plays the ♡4. Partner returns the ♡J, which you take to mean declarer has the ♡Q. Declarer ducks, playing the ♡8, and since you don't want to give up a trick to declarer's queen, you duck as well.

Partner continues hearts, leading the ♡10. Declarer's ♡Q appears and you win with the ♡K; the hearts are blocked because declarer played well. Declarer throws the ◇Q from dummy on this trick.

Does the fact declarer threw the ◇Q from dummy mean he isn't planning to run diamonds because he is missing the ◇A and has the nine tricks he needs from clubs and spades? Or did he drop it because he has five or six or seven top diamonds and the queen has no value to him? What is your guess?

You don't have to guess. Your partner has a count of hearts and knows declarer's ♡Q will fall because your partner has the remaining hearts. She used a suit-preference signal to tell you which suit to lead. She purposely led the ♡10 to the third round of the suit. She could have chosen any of her three hearts: the ♡10, ♡9 or ♡2. Picking the ♡10 tells you the way to her hand is spades. If she wanted you to lead clubs she would have played the ♡2; for diamonds she would have played the ♡9.

Declarer's discard of the ◇Q was designed to sow confusion. Ignore it when your partner has the chance to tell you the real story. Aren't you glad you play with such smart partners?

Here's the whole deal:

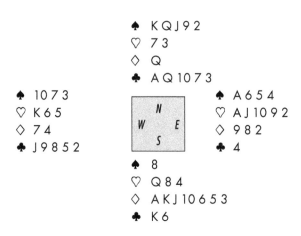

```
              ♠ K Q J 9 2
              ♡ 7 3
              ◇ Q
              ♣ A Q 10 7 3
♠ 10 7 3                        ♠ A 6 5 4
♡ K 6 5          N              ♡ A J 10 9 2
◇ 7 4       W       E          ◇ 9 8 2
♣ J 9 8 5 2      S              ♣ 4
              ♠ 8
              ♡ Q 8 4
              ◇ A K J 10 6 5 3
              ♣ K 6
```

Your heart lead did the trick and partner's suit-preference signal sealed the contract's fate. You scored six tricks and set them two. If you had known partner's holding from the beginning, you could have led a spade at Trick 1 and picked up South's ♡Q on a return heart lead from partner. It is easy to see when looking at all four hands. At the table, you have no reason to assume from the start your partner has the ♠A. Lead a heart and hope it works.

Notice if you start with the 'standard' lead of the ♣5 (fourth highest from your longest suit), or a very passive diamond lead, declarer runs ten tricks off the top before your side can do anything.

We've only scratched the surface of defensive play. Nonetheless, you will be amazed how quickly your scores improve with mastery of these few defensive disciplines.

Have we covered it all: bidding, declarer play and defensive play? Not quite. To this point we have assumed all of our scoring was IMPs, but most pairs games are scored using matchpoints. The next chapter will give you a deeper understanding of how to score well at IMPs. It will also help you understand the modifications you should make in bidding, declarer play and defense when the game is matchpoints.

# Chapter 4:

# PAIRS GAMES VS. TEAM GAMES

So far, we have treated the game of bridge as though it were scored using International Matchpoints (IMPs). Much of the prior discussion is equally valid regardless of how the result is scored. Good bridge is good bridge. However, some decisions can only be made in light of the scoring system used. Since we have been discussing deals scored in IMPs, let's gain a further understanding of that system and then compare and contrast games scored in matchpoints (MPs).

Most team games are scored using IMPs. Most pairs games played in clubs and at tournaments are scored using matchpoints. If you play a lot of online bridge you may play IMP pairs games. However, for simplicity, in this chapter we'll think of team games as IMP games and pairs games as MP games.

In team games you and your teammates play against one other team. You and your partner play (say) North-South at one table and your teammates play East-West at the other table. The team you are playing against sits East-West at your table and North-South at the other table. Once you play the deals at your table, the other table plays the same deals and vice versa. Only the difference in scores between your two tables counts on each deal. These score differences are converted to IMPs using the following table:

| Score Diff | IMPs | Score Diff | IMPs | Score Diff | IMPs |
|---|---|---|---|---|---|
| 0-10 | 0 | 370-420 | 9 | 1500-1740 | 17 |
| 20-40 | 1 | 430-490 | 10 | 1750-1990 | 18 |
| 50-80 | 2 | 500-590 | 11 | 2000-2240 | 19 |
| 90-120 | 3 | 600-740 | 12 | 2250-2490 | 20 |
| 130-160 | 4 | 750-890 | 13 | 2500-2990 | 21 |
| 170-210 | 5 | 900-1090 | 14 | 3000-3490 | 22 |
| 220-260 | 6 | 1100-1290 | 15 | 3500-3990 | 23 |
| 270-310 | 7 | 1300-1490 | 16 | 4000+ | 24 |
| 320-360 | 8 | | | | |

Let's take an example to see how this works. At your table you bid and make a vulnerable game of 4♠ for +620 (good job!). At the other table, on the same cards, the opponents bid 3♠, making four for a score (from your team's perspective) of -170. The net of these two scores is +450 for your team, which translates into +10 IMPs.

On the next deal you again bid and make 4♠ vulnerable for +620. At the other table they bid 4♠ but make an extra trick, so your teammates are -650. The net is -30, and your team gets -1 IMP. The total after two deals is +9 IMPs for the good guys.

This scoring method puts a heavy emphasis on bidding and making games and slams. In the first example the difference between bidding and making 4♠ vulnerable and bidding only 3♠ and making four is 10 IMPs. For a non-vulnerable game the difference is 6 IMPs (420-170 = 250).

When on defense, you are giving your all to defeat the contract. Giving up an overtrick after the contract is made is worth 1 IMP. Setting a game contract that your partners bid and make is worth 11 IMPs non-vulnerable and 12 IMPs vulnerable. If your partners bid three of a major and make, and you set your opponents by 1, the gain declines to 5 IMPs non-vulnerable and 6 IMPs vulnerable.

Bidding and making a small slam in a major compared to bidding game and making two overtricks is equal to the slam bonus (500 non-vulnerable; 750 vulnerable), which converts to 11 or 13 IMPs.

Bidding a small slam in spades and going down one versus bidding 4♠ and making one overtrick is also worth the same 11 IMPs non-vulnerable and 13 IMPs vulnerable (450 + 50 = 500 or 650 + 100 = 750).

Do I expect you to remember all these IMP results? No, but there are a few simple tips to help you out.

## TEAMS TIP #1:
### The main objective is to make or set the contract.

As declarer you should play to guarantee the contract even at the expense of an overtrick or two. For example, let's say you are playing 3NT with this eight-card holding:

K J 7 3

A 8 5 2

Say playing the ace and king safely gives you nine tricks but gives up any hope of overtricks. Finessing for the queen puts the contract at risk, but if it succeeds you'll score two overtricks. You know from Chapter 2 that finessing for the queen is a superior percentage play (over 50%) to playing the ace and king and hoping the queen drops (under 35%). So what should you do?

In a team game, make the contract. Play the ace and king. If the queen falls, so much the better (especially if it falls on your right on the second trick and the finesse would have lost). Always be sure to make your contract first and foremost; overtricks are a bonus. Don't risk an 11- or 13-IMP loss trying to pick up an IMP or two.

Even if your contract is a partscore, say 3♠, your potential gain from overtricks remains the same 1 or 2 IMPs. Although the potential loss should you go down is only 5 or 6 IMPs, it is still clear you should take the money and run.

On defense, play aggressively to defeat the contract even at the risk of allowing overtricks. Let's say your opponents are in 3NT and you consider making a play that sets the contract by one trick if it works; if it fails your defense allows the opponents three overtricks. If you don't try it, they have 3NT on the button. What's the right decision?

The key defensive consideration is to set the contract. Do not do anything to diminish your chances. If your effort fails, you give up three extra tricks for 90 points, which converts to 3 IMPs. If you succeed, you gain 450 (non-vulnerable) or 700 points (vulnerable) for 10 or 12 IMPs. Your play can work less than 25% of the time and still be correct.

In Chapter 3 we looked at a series of situations where East, as defender, had to make a decision about which trick to take with his ace to stop declarer from running dummy's long suit. East needed to make his decision based on count signals given by West. In some of the positions, the signals were ambiguous. In team games, where there is ambiguity, choose the option that has the best chance to defeat the contract.

## TEAMS TIP #2:

### Game: If you sniff it, bid it.

The first time I played a team game was at a Regional in Gatlinburg. With my vast three months' experience, I read up on all the facts about the winning percentages to bid games or slams and my head swam. One of my teammates, Tony Brockman, said, 'It's easy, Jim: if you can sniff game, bid it.' For game contracts that about says it all.

Consider a hand where your choice is to bid a major-suit game or not. You feel confident about nine tricks; the tenth is questionable. For now, let's assume exactly the same declarer play and defense at both tables.

If you and your opponents both make the same decision, the result is a wash. Hey, that's no fun. Instead, let's say you are more aggressive and bid the game and they don't. If you are right, you win 10 IMPs; wrong, and you lose 6 IMPs. If the game makes half the time, you win on average 2 IMPs. If the game only makes just over one-third of the time, you still come out even over the long haul.

Not vulnerable, you win 6 IMPs if you bid and make game, while they stop in partscore. You lose 5 IMPs if you are wrong. The breakeven point is a bit over 45%.

I don't know about you, but with most hands I have no clue during the bidding whether I am stretching to a 40% game or a 50% game. So I'm a little more conservative with non-vulnerable games with their higher breakeven point; but you won't go far wrong if you remember what Tony says and if you sniff a game, bid it.

## TEAMS TIP #3:

### Bid the safest game or partscore.

The difference between bidding and making exactly game in a major suit as opposed to a minor suit or notrump is 1 IMP. Bid the safest game possible. The same goes for partscores. Safety is critical, not the scoring difference between playing in a major or a minor. Remember, your key objective once the bidding is over is to make your contract. Your opponents will try their best to defeat it.

How critical is bidding the safe game? Very. Let's say you are playing a vulnerable deal and can make 3NT all the time. Let's also say you know (I have no idea how you know this, but let's say you do) that if you play the contract in 4♡ you will make it unless there's a really bad trump break. Take the risk of playing the 4♡ and you'll probably earn one additional IMP. If you go down, however, you score -100 for a 12 IMP swing in the wrong direction if the opponents decide to play the safe 3NT.

You need to make that vulnerable 4♡ contract more than 92% of the time for gambling to be the right decision. In a non-vulnerable deal you still have to be right 91% of the time. That's a gamble you should ignore. Bad trump breaks happen surprisingly often, if you look at the probabilities.

Even in partscores, picking the safest contract is good policy. Scoring up three of a major versus three of a minor is worth 1 IMP. Don't stretch to be in a major just because it scores more; choose the minor if you have a better fit.

However, if you can get away with only two of a major and can make it, there is no reason to bid three of a minor to get the same score!

## TEAMS TIP #4:
### Bid 50% small slams.

For small slams the reward for being right and the penalty for being wrong (11 IMPs non-vulnerable and 13 IMPS vulnerable) are the same. Bidding a 50% slam is a neutral proposition. Your opponents are going to bid it; you should too.

Why should you do what the opponents are going to do? Don't you win by doing things differently? Yes, but... which of these situations would you rather be in?

Both you and the opponents bid the small slam, and it makes or it goes down. Either way, the deal is a wash. Everyone shrugs their shoulders: what can you do?

OR...

You didn't bid the slam; the opponents did and made it. You dumped 11 or 13 IMPs. It can be hard to make up that big a deficit.

Of course you can say that it's just as likely when you don't bid the slam that the opponents will go down and you win the 11 to 13 IMPs. Now you're a bright and shining star.

Equally likely, but on average how will you feel? Will being the star because you didn't bid a 50% slam* that went down balance out being the goat when you neglected to bid a makeable slam? Not for me. Sure, I like being the star, but I don't want to be a goat simply because I took a contrary position to the rest of the world on a 50/50 proposition.

## TEAMS TIP #5:
### Bid only 'very confident' grand slams.

The advice I received early on from all sides was not to bid a grand slam in a team game unless you had it cold. At the 2007 Indianapolis Regional, not quite midway through my journey to Life Master, I played in a Knockout against a vastly superior team with two pros whose names you would likely recognize. They bid a grand

---

* This advice only applies if your slam really is 50%. Many players refer to a slam as being 50% when it is actually much less because it depends on both a finesse *and* a trump break — they conveniently assume the trumps will cooperate.

slam. It went down. We won the match because of that one deal. I was convinced
— until I looked at the math.

The difference between bidding a small slam and making an overtrick and
bidding a grand slam is a 500 or 750 bonus for 11 or 13 IMPs. Bidding seven
and going down one compared to bidding six and making is worth 14 IMPs non-
vulnerable and 16-17 IMPs vulnerable (depending on the **strain**). You need to be
correct 55-57% of the time to reach the break-even level. You don't need to be
certain, but it does need to be better than a 50/50 proposition.

However, math does not tell the full story. When you and partner have an
overflowing bucketful of points and a solid trump suit it is likely both you and the
opponents can find their way to slam. In that case, bid the grand. However, if you
expect the slam to make because of distribution — you have a great trump suit but
you are missing a king or a couple of queens in the side suits — even if you are very
confident that you have all the bases covered, it might not be worth bidding the
grand slam because the opponents may not be in any slam!

I recently had an example of this in a pairs game:

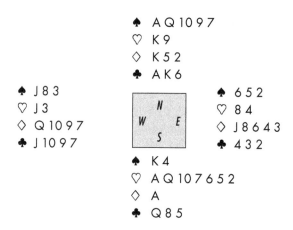

North-South have 'only' 34 HCP, consisting of all the aces and kings and three out
of four queens. South has a seven-card heart suit that runs unless West has four
to the jack, which happens a rare 5% of the time. As the cards lie, the deal is cold
for 7NT, 7♡ and even 7♠ (though no one is likely to choose spades over hearts).
Distribution, not high-card points, makes this grand, and as expected not everyone
found it. Out of twenty-four tables, just four bid the grand slam (all in hearts). Two
pairs could not even stumble their way to any slam! The remaining pairs bid 6♡.

For reasons like the above deal, I want to be very confident (75% or better)
before bidding a grand slam, but I don't need to be certain. Why not follow the
odds here and bid a grand slam that is at least 60%? Because, unless they are
experts, your opponents aren't likely to bid it, and the deficit from going down is
hard to make up with the rest of the deals.

That said, you can take conservatism too far. I played against a pair where the opener bid 2NT (20-21 HCP) and responder had 18 HCP. He only bid 6NT because he couldn't be sure there wasn't duplication in the values somewhere and they would have to lose a trick. With 38-39 HCP, I want to be in a grand slam.

## TEAMS TIP #6:
### Don't double your opponents for an expected one-trick set.

To understand the double-edged nature of doubling (pun intended) look at what happens if you slap down the red X on a vulnerable 2♠ contract. If you set them one, you score +200, twice the +100 you would have scored without the double. That's worth 3 IMPS. A two trick penalty scores up at +500 compared to the +200 without the double. That converts to 8 IMPs.

If you are wrong and they make the contract, they score +670 because you doubled them into game. Compared to the +110 they would get without the double, that mistake costs 11 IMPs. Risking 11 IMPs to score 3 IMPs when you think you can set them one trick is not going to win many friends among your teammates. Even with the potential gain of 8 IMPs you receive for a two-trick set, you'll need to be right almost 60% of the time for the strategy to work.

However, if you are confident of the setting tricks, don't become paralyzed if they have bid too high. The red X isn't just for takeout doubles.

If they are already in game, the downside of being wrong is less negative. For example, doubling a 4♠ contract that makes costs you 4 IMPs. If they make an extra trick the price steepens quickly to 6 or 8 IMPs depending on vulnerability. If they are in game and you believe you can set them by two tricks, you should surely double.

Also, doubling 1NT, 2♣ or 2♦ does not give them game if they make the contract. With these contracts you can be a bit more aggressive with your doubles.

However, don't get too frisky with even 'safe' doubles. Your opponents have a blue XX card in their bidding boxes, and they might just pull it out — especially if they are behind in the match and need a big score for a chance to win.

## TEAMS TIP #7:
### Compete in bidding, but do not be overaggressive, especially when vulnerable.

I was advised early on not to compete strongly in partscore auctions. Following that advice, I lost a number of matches not on missed games but on deals where my opponents made 3♥ at our table and at the other table they made 3♠ on our cards. On that kind of deal we lost 7 IMPs, a worse result than you get by staying out of a non-vulnerable game the opponents bid and make. To win, you need to compete.

I hear you saying, 'Yeah, but what if they go down, isn't that better?' Better than losing 7 IMPs, but not good. For example, at our table they played 3♡ for -140 (from our perspective). At the other table if they played 3♠ down one for +50, our net is -90, still a loss of 3 IMPs.

Remember it is unlikely either side will double the 3♠ bid in a team match, unless you have really overreached, which you should not be doing.

Be aggressive with major-suit bids at the two-level. Generally, your opponents won't double you — it's hard for them to be confident of setting you by two tricks, and they will be reluctant to double you into game at a low level. This does not mean you should get carried away, especially when you are vulnerable and they are not. You should have a decent suit and playing strength, particularly at the two-level and absolutely if you are overcalling in second seat after a strong 1NT opener. Just because your opponents don't double doesn't mean you can't go down, and going down two vulnerable for -200 is likely to be worse than any partscore they could make.

I remember one deal from a Swiss teams event at a Regional against a much stronger team. They were not vulnerable and we were. Dealer, with a balanced 15 HCP, opened 1NT. My partner had five cards each in hearts and clubs and 10 HCP, all in his two suits, and overcalled 2♡, which in our methods showed hearts and a minor. Third hand had 15 HCP and simply doubled for penalty. I had six spades, three hearts and two in each minor and my highest card was an eight. There was nothing I could do but pass and put down the dummy. After the dust settled, our score was -1100. At the other table our partners played 3NT making an overtrick or two for a loss of 11 IMPs. That cost us the match; with a push we could have won.

This is the reason that some people don't like team games. With one big mistake you've ruined the match, and you have to apologize to your teammates. I look at it from a different perspective. If I know I have cost us 11 IMPs on one deal, I know we can get it back because I have three people, instead of only one, who can cover my mistakes!

## THE MATCHPOINT DIFFERENCE

Let's turn now to games scored by matchpoints (MPs). Unlike team games, where the only thing that matters is what happened at your table and one other table, matchpoint scoring takes into account all the tables that played the same cards you did. Your real opponents in matchpoint scoring are the folks sitting in the same North-South or East-West direction as you. As a reminder, we'll refer to these games as pairs games, but understand that not all pairs games are scored this way, just the vast majority.

In matchpoint scoring you receive one point for every pair sitting in your direction that your score beats. You get ½ point for every pair with the exact same score as you. You get a goose egg for each pair that beats you. If there are thirteen pairs all playing the same cards, your maximum score for any board is twelve. That's called a 'top'. The worst you can score is zero, naturally called a 'bottom'.

To get your percentage on a board, divide your score by the maximum. If you scored an 8.5 with a maximum of 12, your percentage is 70.8% — a very good score indeed. To get your overall game score you take your total matchpoints and divide by the maximum per board times the number of boards played. For example, if you played 26 boards, each with a 12 MP maximum, an average game (50%) would be 156 MPs.

So what difference does the scoring method make in how we play the game? Plenty.

Let's look at a deal with eleven pairs. The top score is 10. Both North-South and East-West are vulnerable. The results and matchpoints (MPs) are shown in the table from the North-South perspective.

| Contract | Declarer | Result | N-S score | N-S MPs |
|----------|----------|--------|-----------|---------|
| 4♡ dbld | E | -1 | +200 | 10 |
| 3♠ | N | +1 | +170 | 9 |
| 1NT | N | +2 | +150 | 8 |
| 3♠ | N | = | +140 | 6.5 |
| 3♠ | N | = | +140 | 6.5 |
| 4♠ | N | -1 | -100 | 5 |
| 3♡ | E | = | -140 | 3 |
| 3♡ | E | = | -140 | 3 |
| 3♡ | E | = | -140 | 3 |
| 4♠ dbld | N | -1 | -200 | 1 |
| 6♠ dbld | N | -3 | -800 | 0 |

To get East-West matchpoint scores, subtract the North-South MPs from the maximum MPs, 10. For example, the East-West pairs that bid and made 3♡ got 7 MPs (10 − 3).

Given the scores, we can imagine the deal involved a bidding contest between North-South in spades and East-West in hearts. Note the following:

1) Two of the contracts are wonky. Somehow one North-South pair ended up in 1NT. The East-West pair apparently didn't know Bidding Basic #5: *Learn to compete*, since the bidding stopped there when East-West obviously had a heart fit and some points. If East-West had entered the fray they might have won the auction in 3♡ (three of their fellow East-West pairs did) for a large MPs difference. Even if North-South belatedly found their spade fit, the East-West matchpoints would have climbed from 2 to 3 — not huge, but not nothing either.

2) Presumably the North-South pair who soared to a 6♠ contract that East-West happily doubled made some bidding error(s) along the way.

3) Notice how important an extra trick can be. Whether by great declarer play or inadequate defense, one pair made an overtrick in 3♠ for a next-to-the-top board. That one trick was worth 2 MPs (otherwise there would have been three pairs making exactly 3♠ and each would have scored 7 MPs).

4) One East-West pair took the competitive spirit too far. They overreached to 4♥ and were spanked with a double, earning them a bottom and their opponents a top.

5) Two North-South pairs also overreached with 4♠ bids. One was not doubled and both sides got an average score. The other contract was doubled and that earned East-West a near top of 9 MPs.

6) Every time a North-South pair achieved a positive score they got a better than average result. Similarly, every time an East-West pair got a positive score they also received an average or better result.

How many of these observations are peculiar to this one deal and the pairs playing and how many can be generalized? Let's consider our six observations above.

**1)** In Chapter 1 we discussed the need to compete aggressively when your opponents stop at a low-level partscore. This is even truer at matchpoint scoring than it is at IMPs. Those North-South pairs who sold out to 3♥ scored very poorly.

**2)** The North-South pair in slam deserved a bottom when they ended up so far out of line with other scores.

## PAIRS POINTER #1:

### Avoid doing things that earn bottoms. Don't try for tops; be grateful when you receive them.

I've played with partners who are always trying for tops. While everyone else is playing a nice, secure major-suit game, they try 3NT to see if they can get the extra 10 points. They aggressively double their opponents' partscores. They make nonstandard leads to shake things up. These tactics usually result in a 'pajama game': mostly tops and bottoms. While a rollercoaster ride can be thrilling and you will occasionally earn a big overall score, the steadier approach favored by experts generally works better.

On any given deal there will be pairs who bid poorly and end up in the wrong contract. Some other pairs may misplay the hand and get a suboptimal result. If you are secure in your bidding and get to a good contract, and if you then play your cards well, many more times than not you'll get an above average result based on what should be an average contract and average play. It's all because your steady bidding and play avoids bottoms, and you apply the Declarer Devices and Defensive Disciplines to make the most out of your cards. It's not that you are perfect — you just allow others to make more mistakes.

3) On offense, settling for making your contract is not enough. Every trick counts. Similarly on defense, defeating the contract is not the main goal, if you think they are in a normal spot; the main goal is to take every trick you can, and especially not to concede unnecessary overtricks. A difference of even 10 points in your score can significantly affect your matchpoint result, which means that sometimes you must take risks you would otherwise never take. In our example, the notrump contract (+150) and spade contract (+140) both made nine tricks, but the notrump contract scored an extra 1.5 MPs because of the extra 10 points.

## PAIRS POINTER #2:
### Extra tricks are critical.

Imagine a situation where you and partner find a heart fit and bid a non-vulnerable game. Once dummy's hand comes down you realize most pairs will be in 3NT rather than 4♡, and the 3NT contract is cold for an overtrick. At IMPs, you can make your game and tie with the opponents if they were in notrump. At MP scoring, your goal is no longer to make ten tricks. The competition is going to score +430 in notrump. If you only make your contract, you score +420. In order to get a decent result you must try for an overtrick, even if that risks going down in the 4♡ contract. If you do go down, it may feel bad, but it probably won't cost you much, as you were getting a very poor MP score anyway.

This is a *major difference* between IMP and MP events. At IMPs, there is essentially no difference between scoring 420 and 430. At MPs, 10 points can be the difference between a top and a bottom. At IMP scoring, -1100 can ruin the whole session. At matchpoints, as the saying goes, a zero is a zero; a bottom is a bottom. It doesn't matter how bad a score you got on a particular board, there is no carryover. You dust yourself off and pick up your next hand, and maybe get it back by making an overtrick on that deal.

This emphasis on making an extra trick (or taking an extra defensive trick) has effects that run through everything from bidding to declarer play to defensive play. We'll look at some examples in Chapter 6 where you will determine if you would make the same decisions at IMPs and MPs. (Hint: sometimes you *should* make a different play!)

Well, heck, why not look at an example here? Plop yourself into South's seat. You opened 1NT with both sides vulnerable, partner bid 3NT and West slid the ♡8 onto the table as his opening lead.

♠ K 7 6
♡ 7 6
♦ K 9 6 2
♣ A Q J 9

♠ A J 5
♡ A 10 5
♦ A 8 5
♣ K 6 4 3

It's a notrump contract so you count your tricks off the top and find the contract is in the bag. You have two spades, one heart, two diamonds and four clubs for nine tricks exactly. Is there anywhere else you can score an extra trick? Yes, if the spade finesse is on or West leads them, you can record an extra spade trick. If diamonds split 3-3 you might be able to scratch out another trick with the thirteenth diamond.

East takes the first trick with the ♡Q and after you duck, returns the ♡3. That could be his last heart or he could have started with ♡Q32. You duck again to be on the safe side and West captures the trick with the ♡J. He clears the suit with the ♡9. You pitch a spade from dummy and East discards the ♠2. West started with six hearts, three of which are now good if he gets in.

You run the four clubs. On the third trick East releases another low spade. On the fourth trick East throws a low diamond, and West pitches a low heart. Trying to get a better count on the hand, you cash the top two diamonds. East-West both follow. East played the ♦10 and then the ♦Q. West played the ♦4 and the ♦7. Your remaining cards are:

♠ K 7
♡ —
♦ 9 6
♣ —

♠ A J 5
♡ —
♦ 8
♣ —

West has two hearts and two other cards, either one spade and the ♦J or two spades. East has either four spades or the ♦J and three spades. You have three ways to go:

Alternative 1: Cash the ♠K, then the ♠A, and get a tenth trick if the ♠Q drops.

Alternative 2: Cash the ♠K, then lead low to the ♠J, taking the finesse if the ♠Q does not appear. If West has the ♠Q, he'll cash two hearts for down one. If East has the ♠Q, you score an extra trick.

Alternative 3: Lead a low diamond. If West has the ◊J, you lose that trick and two hearts for down one. If East has the ◊J, he'll have to lead a spade back and you capture two spades and a good diamond for an extra trick.

In IMPs this is a no-brainer. Cash the ♠K, lead toward the ♠AJ and play the ♠A regardless of what East plays. Contract made; next deal please.

In MPs you need to try alternative (2) or (3) depending on your reading of the opponents. What do you know about spades? They either split 5-2 or 6-1. East has the length and is the odds-on favorite to have the ♠Q.

What about diamonds? East pitched one diamond early. Would he do that from Q103? Only if he had to. He's much more likely to have QJ103, and have falsecarded with the queen. But if he had to discard a diamond, it means he was protecting the ♠Q, which we determined he probably has. With three diamonds to the jack, West is going to save the jack and has no reason to give partner count at that stage in the proceedings. He kept two hearts, which are only useful if he can get in.

At MPs I would go for the spade finesse. The odds are very much in your favor and if other people are going to do it, you'll need to match the field for a decent score. Will other people do it? You betcha. Strong players will go through the same kind of analysis you just performed and take the finesse. Weak players always take a finesse, regardless. Either way, most Souths will take the finesse at MPs; so should you.

Here's the complete deal. You can see that either finessing the spade or playing East for the ◊J happens to work, but when you have choices, take the one with the best odds.

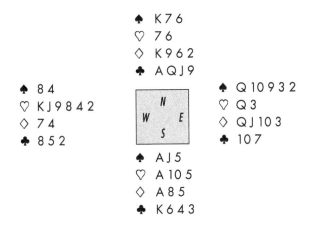

```
                    ♠ K76
                    ♡ 76
                    ◊ K962
                    ♣ AQJ9
    ♠ 84                            ♠ Q10932
    ♡ KJ9842        N               ♡ Q3
    ◊ 74         W     E            ◊ QJ103
    ♣ 852           S               ♣ 107
                    ♠ AJ5
                    ♡ A105
                    ◊ A85
                    ♣ K643
```

Matchpoint scoring can affect not only how you play the hand as declarer, but also your opening lead on defense. For example, if your opponents are in 6NT at IMP scoring, you often make as passive a lead as possible. Unlike leading against 3NT, where you often lead the fourth highest of your longest and strongest suit in hopes of setting up tricks for yourself in that suit later in the play, at 6NT you don't have the luxury of time. This kind of lead in 3NT can even work when the opening lead gives declarer a trick — because it sets up more tricks in your hand. To defeat a 6NT contract you need to take two tricks. The difference between success and failure may depend entirely on not giving up a trick on your opening lead.

Will you always know what the most passive lead is? No, but don't lead away from honors; and if you have a bunch of suits with nothing in them, try leading a suit with three or four small spots since it is slightly less likely that your partner has three or four of them to an honor. Sometimes the bidding indicates the opponents have a solid suit. If so, go ahead and lead it. Remember, the opponents can only lose one trick to set up the twelve that they need. Make them work for it.

At matchpoints, however, you do not always want to lead passively against a 6NT contract. When the bidding indicates they have a couple of long suits to run and you are looking at the ♠A in your hand, you might want to lead it immediately. If you don't lead it at Trick 1, you'll never get it if they can score thirteen tricks from the other three suits. Not taking your ace could yield a very bad board at MPs. At IMPs, if you don't score your ace you lose 1 IMP, whereas if your lead of the ace gives them the contract you have lost 14 or 17 IMPs. At matchpoints, not taking the one trick can result in a bottom — even though taking it will sometimes give the opponents the contract. The better the pair and the more strongly they bid the 6NT, the more likely it is that cashing your ace is the right play. At MPs it's all about hitting singles, not home runs. That's a big difference from IMPs.

## PAIRS POINTER #3:
### Choose the highest scoring game.

Generally, prefer 4♡ and 4♠ (420 or 620) over 3NT (400 or 600) because a trump suit often allows you to score an extra trick. Even though 5♣ or 5◊ score the same as 3NT, usually choose notrump since it is often harder to get the two extra tricks needed to make a minor-suit game contract. (With a glaring weakness in one of the suits, five of a minor may be your only realistic choice.) Also, prefer 3NT over four of a major when both hands are flat and you do not anticipate being able to make tricks by ruffing. Regardless of the contract, you are essentially playing the hand in notrump and should collect the extra 10 points notrump contracts provide.

Please note the words 'generally' and 'often'. These are guidelines rather than absolutes.

## PAIRS POINTER #4:
### Strongly consider doubling whenever you believe your opponents are sacrificing.

Let's go back to our pairs scoresheet and look at observations **4)** and **5)**. Your opponents expect to go down and hope to lose less than if you had played the contract. Doubling reduces the number of tricks you need to set the opponents if you are to recover the score you would have received. In the deal reflected by our scoresheet above, it is clear either side can score +140 if they win the contract at the three-level. Spades is the boss suit and in this case North-South have the advantage. If East-West go to the four-level, North-South have been 'cheated' out of the +140 to which they are entitled. Setting the contract by one trick gives them only +100, and if they don't double they will probably get a below average result. In order to protect their positive score they should consider doubling. If they set the contract by one trick, they score +200 — better than they would have scored playing 3♠.

Will it always work? Nope. Sometimes you double a makeable contract and earn a bottom. Be careful of doubling on freak deals; be aggressive in flat distribution situations where point count gives a better indication of strength.

**6)** A common adage in pairs games is to 'score positive' (i.e. get a positive score). The flip side of this, scoring negative, is generally not a good thing.

To test this out, I analyzed nearly 1,600 deals I played from sixty-five pairs events. I categorized each deal based on the actual score I earned and the MP result based on how others played the same deals. For analysis I grouped the results into six categories:

Category 1: I made a positive score and rated above average compared to others (+/+)

Category 2: I made a positive score and rated exactly 50% compared to others (+/E)

Category 3: I made a positive score, but rated below average compared to others (+/−)

Category 4: I made a negative score and rated below average (−/−)

Category 5: I made a negative score and rated 50% (−/E)

Category 6: I made a negative score, but rated above average (−/+)

If the advice to score positive (and implicitly not to score negative) is true, I should have lots of deals falling into categories 1 and 4. If instead, I found that a higher number of deals fell into Categories 3 and 6 where my results contradicted the adage, then we should ignore the folklore. Categories 2 and 5 are neither fish nor fowl since I received an average result on those boards, but they certainly do not support the proposition.

Drum roll please…

Category 1 (+/+) or Category 4 (-/-)     71.80%
Category 3 (+/-) or Category 6 (-/+)     21.60%
Category 2 (+/E) or Category 5 (-/E)     6.60%

Over 70% of the time you could accurately predict whether I would get an above average or below average MP score based on whether I scored positive or negative.

The rule seems to work for me. Would it for you?

## PAIRS POINTER #5:
### Score Positive.

I'm convinced that scoring positive is the way to go, although we know not all positive scores yield positive MP results.

A typical way to earn a +/- result is to play it 'safe' when deciding whether to bid a game or stop in a partscore. With a fair chance of making the game you'll need to bid it because others will. Bidding three of a major making four, for the dreaded +170, might account for a substantial portion of my +/- results. I have not found the same to be true for slams. Bidding four of a major and making six often still gives you a better than average score, but bidding six and making five is usually ugly (one of those -/- deals).

As your skill increases you should be more aggressive about bidding slams, but I have found playing in the I/N sections of tournaments and against C players at the club that they often overbid to slams and go down more than 50% of the time. Not the A players, but we're not yet up to their level of play.

In partscores, head for a safe contract that scores well. A plus score gets you the points; but in matchpoint scoring you do need to keep in mind the scoring differences between minor suits, major suits and notrump.

## PAIRS POINTER #6:
### Consider doubling in partscore bidding contests
### when you can earn +200.

At IMPs, you learned not to double unless you expected to set them two tricks. At MPs the key consideration is getting as large a positive score as possible. Let's consider an example where we are bidding hearts and they are bidding spades. We bid 3♥, which you are confident we can make; they bid 3♠. We have decent defensive values in our hands. What should we consider at this point?

Did their bidding 3♠ make it any more likely we can make 4♡? Probably not. At IMPs this is an easy decision. Pass and let them play it. Hope we can set them and pick up the next board.

At MPs we have more to think about. If other pairs are allowed to play 3♡ and it makes, they score +140. They are our competition. If we can double our opponents and score at least +200, we'll get a great result because we don't think 4♡ makes. Here's where vulnerability comes into play. If they are not vulnerable, a doubled one-trick set only earns +100, less than the +140 those making 3♡ receive. We need a two-trick set for +300 in order for the double to pay off. How likely is that? You'll need to figure that out, but you probably won't set a 3♠ contract by two tricks very often.

Doubles are not risk-free. If you double the 3♠ contract and it makes, you have given them a top and yourself a bottom. Pairs Pointer #1 suggests we need to avoid bottoms to score well. Could they make 3♠? Sometimes they can make 3♠ while you can make 3♡. The risks for a one-trick non-vulnerable set are usually too high to justify the benefits.

If they are vulnerable, the analysis changes in favor of a double. Now all we need is a one-trick set to earn +200 and score very well on the deal.

Keep this in mind when you are the one with the higher suit and the opponents have the lower. If you are non-vulnerable and reach one level too high and get doubled, you'll still score okay as long as the opponents could make their contract. Be careful if you are vulnerable, and don't become victim to a double that drops you to -200.

To score your best, it is important to keep in mind what type of game you are playing. Some people prefer team events, others prefer pairs. Whichever format you are playing, you can't do it alone. You also need a partner.

# Chapter 5:

## YOU CAN'T DO IT ALONE

I saved this really important chapter for last. If a chapter on partnerships had been first, you probably wouldn't even have bought the book, would you? I thought not. But you are still reading, so trust me and read this chapter carefully. Combine what you have already learned with what you'll learn about partnerships and then head to the bridge table to chart your improvement.

Playing bridge is not a solo activity. You need a partner and two opponents. Much of your success will depend upon whom you choose as your partner. Nothing can ruin a bridge game more quickly than finding yourself stuck with the wrong partner. Believe me, I know.

### THE LECTURER

Eight and a half months into my bridge education, I departed a Regional tournament in total frustration. I had planned to stay for the week, but instead left with three days remaining. During the four days I had been there I had earned fewer than 3 points. At the time I had accumulated a total of 70 masterpoints. My partner, with 500 points, had vastly more experience than I.

My play sucked and was going downhill from there. I was making mistakes I hadn't made since my first month of play. I was frustrated and my partner was equally distressed. What happened?

My partner was a lecturer. Each session provided ample opportunity to point out plays or bids I could have made better. Over lunch or dinner my partner methodically dissected each deal and filled my mind with Help Suit Game Tries and Jordan 2NT bids and Vienna Coups. You may know what all those mean, but at the time I certainly didn't.

I lost faith in my game, and I pressed to find winning plays. I tried to incorporate all the new bidding ideas filling my head. Instead, I found losing lines of play and misbids galore. I tried harder and played worse. Finally my brain shut down. It would not take in any new information and mostly forgot whatever it had once known. I was miserable and went home discouraged.

Whose fault was that awful experience? Surely the lecturer's, you say. Nope. I consider it one of my great learning opportunities and entirely my fault. How so? Wasn't the lecturer the one with experience?

Yes, but I was also responsible for the smooth running of the partnership. My first mistake was not setting ground rules when we agreed to play together. My second was allowing the lecturer to convert me into an incompetent student. In a moment I'll discuss how I've learned to take responsibility for a partnership and what I should have done.

## THE MENTOR

I met John Baity on May 4, 2006 at the Superiorland Bridge Club in Marquette, MI on my second visit to the club. I only knew one person there, gg gordon, who was going to be my partner and was also directing the game. She met me at the door and said she had a 'great' partner for me if I didn't mind the change. 'You two are a lot alike,' she said. 'You'll have a good time.'

John was an experienced player (he had well over 500 points), but he immediately made me feel at ease. He asked to look at my convention card (which was really basic at the time), asked a few clarifying questions and said we could play my card. After we had played each round and were waiting to move to the next table, John chatted with me and the opponents. We talked about everything except bridge. At the end of the session (we took third place out of twelve pairs) he asked me to play again the next week. What fun!

Next week was also enjoyable (this time we finished third out of ten pairs) and we agreed to play again once our schedules matched. Before the next game he asked if I would be interested in learning a different method of signaling with my first discard. I said sure, if he thought there was a better one.

'We'll try it,' he said, 'and you can decide if you like it better.' I concentrated like the devil on first discards that night and we did well, taking first out of eleven pairs. I'm not sure our discards had anything to do with the result. As it happened, that was the only time we came in first. The next day we took a second out of nine pairs. After we were done and agreed to play the following week he asked if I would be interested in learning some 'useful' conventions. Flushed with our success, I said 'Sure', and he gave me a small pamphlet on the Forcing 1NT.

John was a proponent of the **2/1 bidding system** and he planned to introduce me to the full system bit by bit: first adding Forcing 1NTs, next Bergen raises and preemptive raises, and so on. Our lessons ran out at the end of June. John was losing his battle with cancer and no longer had the energy to play. We only played together nine times, but I had the privilege of being his last pupil. That is why I dedicated this book to him.

## THE CRITIC

While Lecturers can jumble your brain with too much information, for the most part they are interested in helping you improve; unfortunately they go about it in the wrong fashion. The critic isn't really interested in your improvement. After a deal is over the critic has a need to show his superiority by letting you know how you could have played better, or led a different card, or what your bidding should have been. The critic is all about self-aggrandizement at someone else's expense.

If you have a thick skin, you might even learn some useful tidbits from this know-it-all, but who needs the aggravation?

If you find yourself partnered with a Critic, after the first instance of discussing your errors at the table, let him know you appreciate his feedback but would prefer to talk about it after the game is over. Once the game is finished, assuming the Critic is still interested in letting you know about your deficiencies without the audience of your opponents, he will probably remember only one or two items and those could actually be useful. If by the end of the game you are simply glad to be done, take a quick trip to the restroom followed by a little chat with the other players, and your Critic will have lost his zeal.

## THE IDEAL PARTNER

A good partner recognizes both your strengths and limitations. Starting out, most of your partners will be more experienced than you. Eventually, you will sometimes be the one with the experience; isn't that scary the first time it happens? Whichever situation you find yourself in, the process of forming a successful partnership should remain the same, and you are responsible. Why *you?*

Who is better equipped than you?

The first time you play with a partner, allow plenty of time to go over your convention card. If the partner is from your club you probably have a good sense of who is the more experienced of the pair, but keep an open mind. If you are at a tournament or the person is a visitor to your club, you may have no idea *a priori* who is the more experienced bidder. When I knew only a few conventions, choosing to play my card was obvious since I knew nothing else. I had no clue what all those other conventions meant and if asked about preferences I would look as blank-faced as a cow in the middle of the field chewing its cud.

In the first few months of playing I learned some more conventions and made the mistake of assuming that agreeing on a convention name meant we agreed on how to bid in the specified situation. After some embarrassing gaffes like: 'Oh, you play Gerber only after a notrump opener. I play it whenever it's obvious,' I finally realized there was a better way to fill out the partnership convention card.

Ask questions. Lots of questions.

If you have a convention card filled out with your preferences, now would be a good time to refer to it. If not, you can find a blank convention card in Appendix A (page 160). Unfortunately, my partner hasn't brought her favorite convention card with her and I can't take a peek before starting my interrogatory.

Me: *Do you usually play Two over One or SAYC (Standard American Yellow Card)?*
P: *2/1, if that's alright with you.*
Me: *Fine. Is 2/1 always game force or —*
P: *Always, and sometimes I open in third seat with only 8 points with a good suit.*

I check the 2/1 Game Forcing box and the one for Very Light Openings, third hand.

Me: *Sounds good. What are your notrump openings?*

P: *1NT is 15-17 and 2NT is 20-21*

Me: *Perfect. Do you play transfers?*

P: *Four-suit transfers.*

Me: *So, after you open one notrump, explain how I let you know to bid diamonds because I have a ton of them and no points.*

P: *Oh, well you bid 2♣; I respond 3♣, and since you want diamonds instead of clubs, you bid 3◊.*

I pat myself on the back for remembering to ask. My partner actually plays a 2♠ relay to 3♣ rather than true four-suit transfers. Even if she really played four-suit transfers we would have to agree on a precise approach.

Me: *Now, what happens if I want to bid 2♡ to transfer you to spades, but they bid 2♡ instead?*

P: *I double for stolen bids.*

Me: *Okay, we can do that. What does it mean if you bid 1NT, they bid 2◊ and I bid 2♡? Is that still a transfer to spades?*

We continue until I make sure I know how we are playing all the bids following a notrump opening with and without interference. Then we move to the majors and quickly agree on five-card majors. The conversation continues until we have covered the convention card, which usually takes twenty minutes at a basic level, but it is well worth the effort.

How many times have you short-circuited the process only to hear the bidding after you open 1◊ proceed (with the opponents passing):

1◊ — 1♠

1NT — 2♣

You go into a trance trying to conjure an image of the convention card you threw together in three minutes, wondering whether your partner plays this 2♣ as conventional, which many do. Or is she just rejecting notrump and offering you a choice of her suits? If you spend the twenty minutes before the game begins, you will know. Why cheat yourself?

Often neither player is clearly the more experienced. Each knows some conventions the other doesn't. Generally you should choose the lower common denominator. Often, the best way to make a less experienced partner comfortable is to use their convention card without modification. As the experienced partner you may have to pay particular attention to conventions you have not used for a long time.

At a short lesson for I/Ns at a national tournament, David Berkowitz was asked about having multiple partners. He thought it was a good idea provided you played the same convention card with each one. He even told the players how to accomplish that. Simply tell your partner that they are most assuredly the better player and then hand them your card to play. A sweet smile should seal the deal with anyone with half an ego (except you of course, since you have been forewarned).

If this hypothetical partner had insisted on teaching me new conventions on the spot, I would have my antenna up wondering whether I had stumbled onto a Lecturer. Even if the person were not a Lecturer, I would wonder if she really wanted a partner in the true sense of the word. I avoid adding anything new to my card if at all possible. If you want, you can try learning one new thing immediately before playing. If you do, both partners should be aware that you are courting a possible disaster or two.

After the game, often while the director is entering the scores in the computer, you and your Ideal Partner will have a few minutes to go over any little bobbles that arose during the course of the play. Maybe one particular bidding sequence was a little unclear to you or perhaps something reminded you of a bidding issue you had not discussed. Sometimes there is a deal where you made your contract, but everyone else made an overtrick and you'd like help in understanding how you could have played the hand better.

How do you remember which deals to talk about? Make notations on your scorecard: *3♡ bid; extra trick; signal*? However you choose to do it, the purpose is to jog your memory. Some clubs and tournaments give you hand records after the game is over, showing all the deals. If hand records are not available, you can go and look at the cards. Often bidding questions can be resolved immediately after playing the boards at a particular table. If not, make sure to wait until the end of play since you don't want to discuss boards your opponents may not have played yet. Play questions should usually wait until after the game has finished.

## THE INCOMPATIBLE PARTNER

After a few times playing with someone you hoped would be an ideal partner, you realize you don't seem to be clicking. You might have run into an incompatible partner. Two good players I know tell this story from a number of years back. Both were decent players and progressing nicely toward their Life Masters. They played tournaments together but were not scoring well. Here's what was happening. One was a more aggressive bidder than the other. The less aggressive of the two pulled back even more to make up for the 'gunslinger' bidding of her partner. This caused the more aggressive bidder to become even more so to make up for the 'timidness' of her partner.

It doesn't take much imagination to see those combined reactions to each other's bidding styles spiraling down to where neither one could trust the other's bidding. Happily, they were able to recognize the problem and fix it. They agreed to bid their own hands with no 'extra' adjustments and everything righted itself.

Maybe different styles of bidding are causing your poor performance. Maybe your partner cannot play at your level. Wait, I hear you say. I don't want her to play at *my* level. I need her to play at *her* level, or even better, to make up for my inexperience.

Only partly true. You want your partner to play her best as declarer. Similarly, you want her to use her experience in evaluating whether to bid an iffy game or slam. However, she also needs to recognize who will be playing the hand.

Playing an iffy slam, she may have better than a 50% chance because she has at her command a solid arsenal of endplays, squeezes, coups, etc. to see her through. If you are playing the slam, you may only have a 25% chance based on your current knowledge of advanced declarer play. Does that mean your experienced partner should never bid an iffy slam or game? Of course not, but if you continually find yourself playing and going down in contracts only the club experts can make, maybe your partner needs to reevaluate her bidding *when playing with you.*

Similarly, your more experienced partner has to think at your level while playing defense. If your knowledge does not yet include suit-preference signals, it does no good — and often great harm — for your partner to make such signals or to interpret your cards as suit preference. If she remembers your lack of experience, she will not expect you to make plays based on knowledge you don't have and will adjust her play to what you are actually doing, not what she would do in your shoes.

If 'misunderstandings' continue, it might be time to look for a new partner for your next game and perhaps return to this partner once you have learned a bit more.

## MULTIPLE PARTNERS (GOOD OR BAD?)

There are advantages to having a single partner. Over time your partnership will develop a thorough understanding of your bidding and defensive play that partnerships with fewer games played together cannot duplicate.

For me, having multiple partners provides many more advantages than playing with only one other person. To be honest, when I first began playing, the only people who might have been interested in being my steady partner probably didn't know much more than I did. For me, making progress when the blind leads the blind is frustratingly slow. But if your disposition is different from mine, that might work well for you.

Finding one good mentor and sticking with them to the exclusion of other partners may not be the best long-term approach for several reasons. The bidding system your mentor knows and teaches may not be best suited for you. Over time, the more different approaches you are exposed to the better able you are to choose what works well for you. Furthermore, the more approaches you are exposed to, the better you can understand (and possibly thwart) the opposition. Lastly, different players have different strengths: one partner may explain the risk and rewards of very light preempts in a way that is clearer to you, while another does a better job in explaining how to use responsive doubles.

Having multiple partners can also have its downside. David Berkowitz's ploy for getting everyone to play your current convention card is not a cure-all for the problem of playing different systems with different people. Playing too many different things can slow down your learning process because instead of concentrating on what you are trying to learn, you are spending lots of energy remembering which conventions you are playing today, what discard system you are using and whether this is the partner who insists on MUD opening leads.

Because I split my time between summer and winter residences, I don't really have a choice. While earning my 300 points to become a Life Master, I played with fifty-one different individuals, not counting Internet play. Some like John Baity were Mentors and Ideal Partners; others were either Incompatible Partners, Critics or Lecturers. Sometimes I purposely play with Critics and Lecturers because I want to learn something specific from them and it's worth the extra aggravation.

As I gained experience I found myself playing more often with less experienced partners. I had to learn to keep my newfound knowledge to myself and not become a Lecturer or a Critic. If I learned something new, I nearly burst with enthusiasm to share my bounty. If you are like me, count to twenty — twice — before offering up your wisdom. Then maybe people will find you to be an Ideal partner.

## LAST WORD ON PARTNERSHIPS

When you've finished your session, put on your best smile and thank your partner. They took several hours out of their finite life to play with you. If that isn't worth a little thanks, what is?

# Chapter 6:

# TRY THESE

In this chapter are a baker's dozen problems to test your bidding and playing skill. Some of the problems have a single question for your consideration. Others describe a line of play and ask you specific questions at various points in the action.

When I work through bridge problems I have a pencil and eraser in hand to put tick marks next to cards as I play them so I can see what still remains. Feel free to do the same.

## PROBLEM 1

North-South vulnerable, sitting West you pick up

♠9 4   ♡A 7 3   ◇A J 8 5 3   ♣8 6 4

The bidding proceeds as follows:

| West | North | East | South |
|------|-------|------|-------|
| pass | 1♣ | pass | 1♠ |
| pass | 2♠ | pass | pass |
| ? | | | |

They stopped in a 2♠ partscore. This is a typical situation you'll encounter at the table. You have 9 HCP and one point for length. **Do you pass or bid?** Do you have a different answer if the game is scored in IMPs or MPs?

**IMPs:** In general, you've learned to hate to let the opponents play in two-level contracts, but whether you like it isn't the question. The question is whether you should bid and if so, what? Your only choices with this hand are a really ugly double (my partners always show up with 3-3-2-5 distribution and I end up playing a 3-3 heart fit because they assume I have four) or bidding 3◇.

Let's reject the double and consider what can happen in 3◇. Best result is when 2♠ and 3◇ both make. You gain 220 points (the +110 they would have gotten making 2♠ and the +110 you got by bidding and making 3◇), which translates into 6 IMPs. If 2♠ makes, but you go down one, you've saved 3 IMPs and if you go down two, you have a wash (-100 and -110 score the same at IMPs).

Sometimes you'll push them to 3♠, which they can't make, and score a 5-IMP swing. Other times you'll push them to a game they can make, because after your bid, North may reevaluate his hand. Then you turned -170 into -620 and a 10-IMP disaster. I've seen it happen more than once.

If it turns out they have the cards to double 3◊ and you go down the expected two tricks, your bid gave them an extra 190 points (300 for the two trick set less the 110 they could have earned). That disaster is worth 5 additional IMPs to the bad guys and if they happen to set you three doubled, you've tossed away 9 IMPs.

Other possibilities occur in the middle, but the short story is you only know they have a spade fit and they don't think they have game. Bidding 3◊ at IMP scoring is taking on more risk than the meager rewards justify. Let them play this one.

**MPs**: The balance of risk/reward changes at matchpoints. They have the majority of the points, so their objective is a maximum plus — which they've decided they can get with a partial spade contract. When they have the points, your objective changes to minimizing your losses (not that you'll eschew a plus score if you can get one). If you don't intervene, you will almost certainly score negative. By bidding 3◊ (let's continue to agree a reopening double here is not pretty) you face the following changed results:

| Good things happen | Your score (compare this to the -110 you get if they make 2♠) |
|---|---|
| You make 3◊ | +110 |
| You go down one | -50 |
| You go down 2 | -100 |
| You go down 1 doubled | -100 |
| You push them to 3♠ and set them one | +100 |
| **Bad things happen** | |
| You go down two doubled | -300 |
| You push them into a makeable game | -620 |
| **Ho hum** | |
| You push them to 3♠, which they were going to make anyway | It's a wash |

At IMPs you must worry about the size of the bad results. At MPs you decide based on frequency. While both bad results at MPs will probably earn you bottoms, the good results happen much more frequently, and all of them improve your matchpoint score. If you happened to go down three doubled for -500, in all likelihood it won't be any worse for you than going down two doubled for -300. A zero is a zero; a bottom a bottom.

At matchpoints, bid 3◊. They had an almost sure positive score before you bid; the pressure is now on them. Let's see how they respond.

## PROBLEM 2

Sitting North with East-West vulnerable you pick up this dandy collection

♠ A 9 8 5  ♡ K 10 8 6 2  ♢ A 2  ♣ 9 5

and the bidding proceeds:

| West | North | East | South |
|------|-------|------|-------|
|      |       | 1♢   | pass  |
| 1♡   | pass  | 1NT  | pass  |
| pass | ?     |      |       |

You have 11 HCP and one point for length — that is if you count length in a suit your opponents already bid. **What's your bid playing IMPs? Playing matchpoints?**

The opponents stopped at 1NT, suggesting that the points on this deal may be split fairly evenly between the two sides. Partner couldn't find a bid even though she has points and shortness in hearts. Unfortunately for you, they began the bidding and have the advantage. You want to compete but are stuck for a bid. You don't have a suit to bid since West already bid your hearts (although you like your K10 sitting behind West). If you double, you know beyond any doubt South will bid one of the minors, although your partner is allowed to pass and defend against a 1NT doubled contract.

At IMPs, this is one of those situations where it is probably better to pass.

At MPs, if they can make their 1NT contract, you will usually end up with a poor result. Even if you go down one, you'll improve your score, and if the opponents bid at the two-level they may be the ones going down. Given your values and lack of a suit, double is your preferred matchpoint bid.

Here's the whole deal:

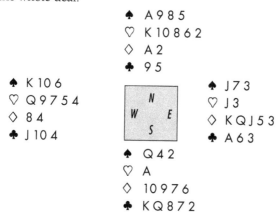

♠ A 9 8 5
♡ K 10 8 6 2
♢ A 2
♣ 9 5

♠ K 10 6
♡ Q 9 7 5 4
♢ 8 4
♣ J 10 4

♠ J 7 3
♡ J 3
♢ K Q J 5 3
♣ A 6 3

♠ Q 4 2
♡ A
♢ 10 9 7 6
♣ K Q 8 7 2

In the actual deal, I was sitting West. North passed us out in 1NT, catching my partner with a minimum opener and me with a minimum response. The majority of the points were in North-South and we went down three for +300 for North-South (with more precise declarer play we could have held it to down one).

If North reopens the bidding with a double, South's best approach is to pass (and should do so at IMPs as well, if North decides to double).

## PROBLEM 3

Both sides vulnerable and from the same pairs game, sitting East you pick up

♠ J 7 4 2   ♡ 8 7   ◇ A K J 7 3 2   ♣ 3

and hear North pass. **Do you bid or pass?**

With 9 HCP and two points for length, I didn't think I had quite enough for a 1◇ opener. At the time I played this hand, I followed the 'rule' that you don't preempt in second seat if you also hold a four-card major. Therefore I passed. (If you did something different, hang in there; you might have made the better call.) South opens a 15-17 1NT, which is passed around to you.

| West | North | East | South |
|------|-------|------|-------|
|      | pass  | pass | 1NT   |
| pass | pass  | ?    |       |

**Do you reopen and, if so, what do you bid?**

Here is the thinking process I used when I faced this situation. South has 15-17 HCP. North probably has a flattish hand (since he didn't transfer) and fewer than 8 points (since he didn't explore bidding game). North-South have at most 24 points, leaving my partner at least 7, all sitting behind the 1NT bidder. North-South have flat hands and I expect my partner to have a couple of diamonds to support me. I bid a natural 2◇. I thought I had a reasonable shot at making the contract, and if nothing else it gave my partner a good lead if North-South ended up in 2NT, which they did.

Let's turn to the play of the hand. Your partner got the hint and led the ◇8 against the 2NT contract. Dummy is displayed:

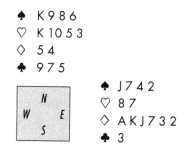

```
        ♠  K 9 8 6
        ♡  K 10 5 3
        ◇  5 4
        ♣  9 7 5
                          ♠  J 7 4 2
              N           ♡  8 7
        W           E     ◇  A K J 7 3 2
              S           ♣  3
```

South immediately calls for the ◇4. Don't be pushed around; stop and reflect.
**What do you play?**

Dummy shows 6 HCP, you have 9 and declarer has 15-17, leaving your partner 8-10. With that many points your partner should score a trick or two during the play.

Consider what you know about the diamond suit. The ◇Q1096 are missing. Declarer bid 1NT and therefore should have two, three or four of the remaining diamonds. That leaves partner with two, one or zero remaining. Your partner read Chapter 3 and makes standard leads.

Given the lead of the ◇8, if partner started with either ◇Q108 or ◇Q98, you can run off six diamond tricks by sticking in the ◇J and cashing the ◇AK.

If partner has a doubleton, it must be the ◇86, leaving declarer the ◇Q109. You can't take all six diamond tricks, but as soon as partner wins a trick she can lead her ◇6 and you can rattle off five diamond tricks. To do that, you must play low on the first trick to force South to take that trick. If you play the ace or king, taking the first trick, and then drive out South's queen, your partner won't have any diamonds left to lead once she wins a trick. That's why it is critical to force declarer to take the first diamond trick.

If partner has a singleton ◇8, after the game is over suggest she reread the section in Chapter 3 about opening leads, since leading a singleton against notrump usually does not work out well. In all likelihood you'll score your ◇AK near the end of play, and those will be the only two diamond tricks you take regardless of whether you play your top diamonds early or late.

Remember to thank your partner for making a standard lead that helped you understand the diamond suit and allowed you to correctly duck the diamond first trick.

Here's the whole deal:

```
                    ♠ K 9 8 6
                    ♡ K 10 5 3
                    ◇ 5 4
                    ♣ 9 7 5
  ♠ 10 3                          ♠ J 7 4 2
  ♡ A Q 9 4          N            ♡ 8 7
  ◇ 8 6          W       E        ◇ A K J 7 3 2
  ♣ Q J 10 6 4       S            ♣ 3
                    ♠ A Q 5
                    ♡ J 6 2
                    ◇ Q 10 9
                    ♣ A K 8 2
```

What actually happened: The 2NT contract went down one for +100 to the good guys. Notice with decent defense North-South can defeat 2◇ by one trick and give us a -100 score. Had I not bid, they would have played and made 1NT for -90. Was competing with my 2◇ bid wrong because it could have resulted in a worse result than if I had let them play in 1NT?

I don't think so. One of the reasons to compete in the bidding is to put pressure on your opponents. When I did that with the 2◇ bid, South had to pass. He had already bid his hand fully, and from his perspective, North could have a bust hand with no points. My partner wisely did not try to find a better fit and smoothly passed. The pressure was on North, who knew his side had a majority of the points (21-23). He thought he didn't have particularly good defensive values against diamonds and was unwilling to let us steal the hand, so he bid 2NT. Good bids do not always work, but they do work more often than not. Make the 2◇ bid.

Let's go back to the original decision not to bid 2◇ at my first chance. The value of preemptive bids is to put pressure on the opponents. Should I have let the four spindly spades stop me from preempting 2◇? When deciding whether to preempt, it is important to consider bidding position. In first seat, the chances are twice as likely your preempt gets in the way of the opponents rather than partner. In third seat, partner has already passed, so you are only inhibiting free bidding by the opponents. In second seat it's a fifty-fifty proposition.

One risk of preempting with my hand is that we miss a spade fit — maybe even game. At matchpoint scoring, making some number of tricks in a major can be worth a lot of matchpoints compared to making the same number of tricks in a minor.

After a 2◇ opening, South has a standard 2NT bid (showing his strong 1NT hand and a stopper in diamonds). In this deal, North will pass, and we should get the same result. However, on a different deal if South had a 15-point notrump and North had an extra king, without the preemptive 2◇ bid, North would invite and they would stop in 2NT, sometimes making 9 tricks. After the preempt, North can no longer invite and might just bid game. Sometimes we will set them an extra trick, but sometimes they make a game they would never have bid. At matchpoints that might be an acceptable tradeoff. At IMPs, it could be a disaster.

On balance, even at matchpoints, opening this hand 2◇ vulnerable in second seat has too much risk for too little reward. If you are sitting in third seat, then by all means bid 2◇. If you use 2◇ for a conventional bid, then you should even consider opening 3◇ (subject, of course, to partnership agreements.)

## PROBLEM 4

With neither side vulnerable in a club pairs game, sitting North you pick up this potential opener

♠Q  ♡Q632  ◇A7  ♣KQ8743

only to hear your RHO open 1♣ and your LHO pipe up with, 'Could be short'. West stole your bid; you have no other good bid, and therefore pass.

| West | North | East | South |
|------|-------|------|-------|
| 1♣¹ | pass | 2♠² | pass |
| pass | ? | | |

1. Could be short.
2. Alerted as a weak jump shift.

After East's weak 2♠ is passed to you, **what do you bid?**

I hate these kinds of hands. In my gut I'm pretty sure we have a majority of the points. With a singleton in spades, 11 useful HCP (the ♠Q is probably worthless) and four hearts, maybe your side should be playing in hearts. You could double and hope your partner bids hearts. (Of course, mine always bid diamonds…) Or with your six clubs you could bet West only had two or three clubs for their 'could be short' 1♣ bid. Then your partner perhaps has two or three or even four to go with your six. Maybe you should toss out a 3♣ bid.

All these choices are ugly. I'd stew and then pass. However, if you choose to double (as the player with your cards did) the bidding continues:

| West | North | East | South |
|------|-------|------|-------|
| 1♣¹ | pass | 2♠² | pass |
| pass | dbl | pass | 3◇ |
| pass | ? | | |

**Now what?**

North concluded after the 2♠ bid that East-West might be stealing. He chose to double, hoping his partner wouldn't choose his two-card diamond suit — which, of course she did. After the diamond bid, North needs to keep in mind *fully bid your hand, but only once* and *when you have a misfit, pass.* North should pass.

Let's now give you West's hand and play it out, assuming South ends up in 3◇.

$$♠2 \quad ♡K95 \quad ◇KQJ5 \quad ♣A10962$$

**What will you lead?** (Note to North: good thing you didn't try bidding clubs, eh?)

You have a singleton in your partner's suit — spades. Why look any further? Wise guy in the back row answers: because this is a bridge book and we want to examine all the possibilities before making a decision. When sitting at the table, it's also right to consider your alternatives before making the 'obvious' choice.

Your partner's 2♠ bid only promised six spades and said nothing about the strength of the suit. So leading a spade because it is her bid suit has a little less meaning than if she had made a stronger bid. The reason to lead a singleton is often to get a future ruff. If South has the ◇A, then you have three natural trump tricks with your ◇KQJx sitting behind the ◇A. But North is the one who entered the bidding fray with the double. If he has the ◇A, then ruffing a spade could capture a third diamond trick.

What about leading hearts? Partner's 2♠ bid should mean she has at most one honor in outside suits. There is no reason to suspect her (possible) one honor is the ♡A or ♡Q. It's much more likely that leading hearts may cost a trick.

How about diamonds? With the ◇KQJx holding you can do a good job of drawing trumps for declarer. But, remembering the discussion in Chapter 3 about when leading a trump is advisable, you realize none of the criteria fit this situation. So not diamonds.

Clubs? Lead away from the ace? Wash your brain out if you considered that. Lead the ace? Almost as bad. This bidding doesn't suggest you need to hurry to open the club suit and ignore partner's bid.

Looks like the ♠2 wins hands down. Here's the full deal:

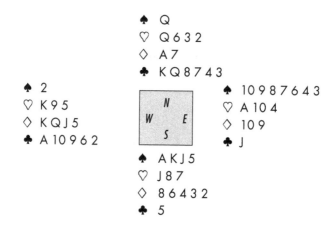

```
              ♠ Q
              ♡ Q 6 3 2
              ◇ A 7
              ♣ K Q 8 7 4 3
  ♠ 2                          ♠ 10 9 8 7 6 4 3
  ♡ K 9 5          N           ♡ A 10 4
  ◇ K Q J 5    W      E        ◇ 10 9
  ♣ A 10 9 6 2     S           ♣ J
              ♠ A K J 5
              ♡ J 8 7
              ◇ 8 6 4 3 2
              ♣ 5
```

Well, shoot. Looking at all four hands, it's clear that leading either hearts or the ♣A can set the contract by three tricks because of East's club ruff. Leading the ♠2 only allows East-West to set the contract two tricks for a score of +100. If North hadn't made a speculative double, East-West would make their 2♠ contract, earning them +110. Unfortunately, North did reopen the bidding with a double, and because West made the 'right' lead, East-West only scored +100 and got a bad matchpoint result.

It happens all the time. You got fixed. Maybe North took the 'learn to compete' mantra a bit aggressively with his double, but it worked out well for North-South and not so well for East-West this time.

But not at the table when this deal played. Here's what actually happened: North committed a major faux pas. Violating the bidding rules about not bidding values twice and not trying to correct a misfit, North bid 4♣ over 3◇. Who knows why West didn't double the contract, but after the dust cleared, East-West set that contract by four tricks, giving them a +200 and a top.

Not all reopeners are going to work out, but you court disaster if you reopen without the shape and/or values for your bid and also continue bidding past the level your hand can support.

## PROBLEM 5

You are sitting South in this deal. With the bidding shown below, you end up in a 3NT contract. West leads the ◊Q. **Plan your play assuming IMP scoring.**

| West | North | East | South |
|------|-------|------|-------|
|      |       | pass | 1♠ |
| pass | 2♣[1] | pass | 2NT |
| pass | 3NT   | all pass | |

1. Game force.

♠ Q 8
♡ A K
◊ A 8 7 6
♣ A 8 6 5 2

♠ A K 7 3 2
♡ Q J 6 4
◊ K 4
♣ 9 7

It's a notrump contract, so count your winners. If you unblock dummy's hearts and manage your entries between the hands, you have ten tricks off the top: three spades, four hearts, two diamonds and one club. Nothing can jeopardize the contract unless you do it yourself.

Your side has 30 HCP, leaving them only 10 HCP. Normally in notrump, a lead of an honor in a suit not bid by partner indicates a sequence of at least three. For now, let's place the ◊QJ10x(x)(x) in West's hand. You have a second stopper in diamonds, so regardless of the actual holdings, you can afford to give up the lead once in trying to set up additional tricks.

With the contract secure, you turn your attention to developing additional tricks. Recalling that *length makes strength*, you consider your long suits. Perhaps you can develop a trick or two from your spade and club suits, each of which has five cards in a single hand and seven cards between the two hands. Spades is clearly the stronger suit and it makes sense to explore them first and keep a stopper in clubs should you lose the lead. The bidding and opening lead provide no additional information about spades, so it's time to make a decision: **are you going to win the diamond lead in dummy, in hand, or duck it?**

With a second stopper in diamonds and only one stopper in clubs, you want to take this trick rather than see them shift to a club and knock out your ace before you have had a chance to establish your hoped-for extra spade winners.

If you answered, 'in dummy with the ◇A', your play can proceed as follows. Next cash the ♡A, ♡K and ♣Q, lead a low spade toward your hand and take it with the ♠A. As long as spades break no worse than 4-2 (an excellent 84% chance) you are guaranteed eleven tricks. Play the ♠K and find out if it is really your lucky day and both opponents have three spades (a fair 36% chance). They don't, so lead one more spade, which East captures. Whatever East leads, you can win the next trick. If East leads a club, win in dummy and lead a diamond to your ◇K (the reason you took the first trick in dummy) and then cash your two hearts and remaining spade.

If you decided to take the first trick in your hand, you lost needed transportation to capture more than three spade tricks unless spades break 3-3. Cash the ♠Q, and unblock hearts by taking the ♡A and ♡K. Lead a low spade back to your hand, taking the ♠A and ♠K. You now discover spades split 4-2 and your suit won't run. Since you may never get back to your hand, cash the ♡Q and ♡J. You can take the aces of clubs and diamonds for ten tricks.

I cut you a break and made this an IMP deal, so if you played it wrong, it only cost you 1 IMP for your lost trick. However, even when you are playing a team game, think carefully about developing a plan for extra tricks *once you have secured your contract*. Had this been scored at matchpoints, that extra trick would probably be the difference between an **average-plus** and **average-minus** score.

Here's the whole deal:

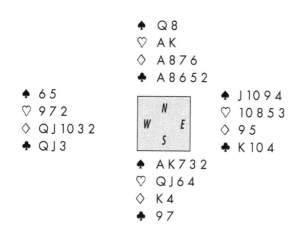

```
                    ♠ Q 8
                    ♡ A K
                    ◇ A 8 7 6
                    ♣ A 8 6 5 2
    ♠ 6 5                          ♠ J 10 9 4
    ♡ 9 7 2          N             ♡ 10 8 5 3
    ◇ Q J 10 3 2  W     E          ◇ 9 5
    ♣ Q J 3          S             ♣ K 10 4
                    ♠ A K 7 3 2
                    ♡ Q J 6 4
                    ◇ K 4
                    ♣ 9 7
```

## PROBLEM 6

You are sitting South in a pairs game with both sides vulnerable. You sort your cards

♠Q 10  ♡ 10  ◇J 10 9  ♣A K J 10 8 7 3

and are wondering what to bid, only to hear your RHO open 1NT (15-17 HCP).

| West | North | East | South |
|------|-------|------|-------|
|      |       | 1NT¹ | ?     |

1. 15-17 HCP.

**Given whatever methods you use to compete over a strong notrump, what do you bid?** If you use different methods with different partners, consider what you would bid under each method, and why.

If (1) you pass and (2) they stay in notrump and (3) your partner happens to have the ♣Q or either opponent has it singleton or doubleton, then you have the first seven tricks and their contract goes down. Even if RHO has Qxx, you get all your clubs as long as you can find a way to partner's hand. Of course, if East-West end up in hearts or spades, your hand's defensive value drops to maybe a trick or two.

Early in my playing experience I would pass and pray. Marty Bergen named his system for bidding after the opponents open 1NT 'DONT', which stands for Disturbing Opponents' NoTrump. Part of the reason for bidding is to find a contract you and your partner can play; part is to get your elbows out and disturb your opponents' bidding!

In a matchpoint game, you need to go with the percentages, and these days with this type of hand I make my bid and interfere with my opponents' auction. When this deal was actually played, we were using a method where 2♣ was not a natural bid, and I chose to bid 3♣.

After my bid, everyone else passed. I had certainly disturbed the opponents. Now I had to bring the contract home. West led the ♠2 and dummy came down:

♠  A 9 8 6 3<br>
♡  K 7 6 5<br>
◇  7 6 4<br>
♣  5

♠  Q 10<br>
♡  10<br>
◇  J 10 9<br>
♣  A K J 10 8 7 3

**Plan your play before you read on.**

You note the bridge gods have maintained their sense of humor and provided your partner with only one club, leaving five outstanding. The good news is you are unlikely to get a 5-0 split, but if you do, it's the notrump hand to your right that has them (since his notrump bid promises at least two). Your losers include a spade, a heart, three diamonds and zero, one or two clubs depending on the distribution.

If West was kind enough to lead away from the ♠K, you can now score two spade tricks. If West has the ♡A and does not go up with it at the first lead of hearts from your hand, you should avoid the heart loser. If you can corral the ♣Q, you might escape with no club losers.

Your side has 18 HCPs; East has 15-17 HCPs. West has only 5-7 HCPs, so without interference, he would either pass or transfer to a major. They might be able to make two hearts, but given partner has the ♠A, chances are good you would set them in a 1NT contract by two tricks for a +200 score.

Nothing you can do in a 3♣ contract will score +200. Your bid (well, my bid if you insist) is a loser relative to defending their notrump. That means you need to concentrate on scoring better than tables where East-West are playing in a heart contract. If they make 2♡, other North-South pairs will score -110. That's what you need to beat, and down one will do it with a -100 score. This didn't work out as you planned, but it's time to *love the one you're with*.

So here's what I did. I ducked the opening lead in dummy and lost to the ♠K. East, hoping to give his partner a ruff, led back the ♠7. I played the ♠Q from hand since following suit is generally a good idea, and West donated the ♠4. Before playing from dummy, I thought about the hand again. The opponents were playing standard count. I tried to figure out the spade holding. The ♠J5 were still missing. If East had them both, West should have started with the ♠4 and then played the ♠2 on the second trick, showing a doubleton. If West had both cards, East leading the ♠7 made some sense. From the play of the first trick, he might have thought declarer had three spades and hoped to get a future ruff if his partner got the lead before trumps had been pulled.

With the ♠K75, East might also have led the ♠7, showing his partner he had one more spade remaining. But why would East risk the possibility of declarer having the ♠J, West the ♠Q and setting up a good spade in dummy that could be used to pitch one of declarer's losers, when he could immediately attack diamonds? I concluded East held a doubleton spade. West knows the count and by playing the ♠4, West is giving East the count.

I sorted through that in a bit less time than it took to write this analysis and decided to leave a spade stopper in dummy in case they were led again; plus being in my hand allowed me to lead toward the ♡K immediately to try to steal a heart trick if West had the ♡A and ducked.

Talk about thinking about the wrong things! Without yet knowing what West's hand is, let's drop into his mind for a moment. He knows dummy has 7 HCP and his partner has 15-17 HCP. Given his own HCP, he can figure out I have 9-11, of which he has already seen two when I played the ♠Q, leaving 7-9 HCP. Since North-South are vulnerable, he figures I must have at least 5 HCP in clubs and more likely 6-8 HCP to bid 3♣ over a 1NT opener, leaving not much in hearts or diamonds. He also assumes I hold six to eight clubs, say seven on average; he knows I have two and only two spades. He concludes I probably have four cards in diamonds and hearts.

If he has the ♡A, he has no reason to duck the first round. He'll jump up with the ace and switch to diamonds, allowing the bad guys to cash all their diamond tricks — in this case three. Eventually I'll have to ruff something in hand and lead out the ♣AK, hoping the ♣Q drops for down one. More likely with a 3-2 trump split, I'll be down two for the terrible -200 score I wanted to avoid — which is what happened, as the full deal was:

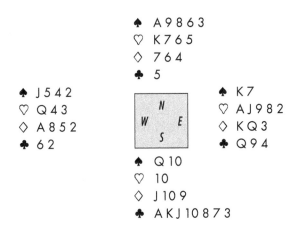

```
                    ♠ A 9 8 6 3
                    ♡ K 7 6 5
                    ◇ 7 6 4
                    ♣ 5
    ♠ J 5 4 2                          ♠ K 7
    ♡ Q 4 3           N                ♡ A J 9 8 2
    ◇ A 8 5 2    W         E           ◇ K Q 3
    ♣ 6 2             S                ♣ Q 9 4
                    ♠ Q 10
                    ♡ 10
                    ◇ J 10 9
                    ♣ A K J 10 8 7 3
```

What I should have been concentrating on was eliminating the club loser and, given East's 1NT opening, it's likely the ♣Q is in his hand. The only entry to dummy is the ♠A. If I duck the first spade trick, I can lose the second to a ruff if East happens to have opened 1NT with a five-card spade suit. Then I have managed two spade losers *and* killed my only sure entry to dummy to take a club finesse.

I neglected to consider not only what I can learn from dummy, but what the defense can figure out. I did not need to take extreme measures to make my contract. I had already decided I needed to make sure I didn't go down two, and that should have been my focus.

My best shot at down one was to minimize the club losers, which means I needed to visualize East holding ♣Qx or ♣Qxx so the finesse would work. I should have won the opening lead with the ♠A and immediately taken the club finesse. On the layout it works and I hold the losers to one spade, one heart and three diamonds. Down one.

Part of your matchpoint planning process should be to determine what your minimum goal is, given where the rest of the field will be. On this deal my objective should have been down one. To accomplish that goal, I needed to draw trumps immediately. Because I only had one trump in dummy, I couldn't play the ace first and then take the finesse to maximize my odds of success. Still, the 50% finesse is better than the 35% chance of dropping the queen by playing the ace and king. (See the discussion following Declarer Device #6 if you don't remember those numbers.)

Would anything have been different at IMPs? For starters, let's go back to my bid. At matchpoints, the frequency of results shapes your course of action. If (as I probably did) you earn a zero on one board, you can still recover. At IMPs the tradeoffs change. The best case is that they can make their 1NT and I can make 3♣. Then my bid earns me 5 IMPs. If they were going down two and now I go down one, I've lost 7 IMPs. Also, if West has the rest of the points and doubles, I'll take only six tricks for -800, and I'll have given them a huge IMP gift. And if I don't win the contract, my bid may give declarer enough information to make a contract that otherwise might have failed.

There are too many bad results to justify the possible small gain at IMPs. Regardless of your methods, pass is preferable. But if you did bid 3♣, then you must take every possible chance to try to make the contract.

Alas, little in our prior analysis changes. It is now worth ducking from dummy on Trick 1 in hopes of scoring the ♠Q, but after East wins that trick with the ♠K, I need to win the spade return in dummy and take the club finesse. After clubs are cleared, it's worth giving your opponents the opportunity to make a mistake, so lead up to the ♡K and hope to steal the ninth trick. However, unless West is asleep, he too knows it's the ninth trick and will go up with the ♡A and mow down your diamond losers.

Any way you look at it, this was not one of my shining moments. Next deal?

## PROBLEM 7

Neither side is vulnerable in this deal from a matchpoint pairs game. Sitting South you hold

♠KJ532 ♡Q1043 ◇J ♣QJ6

and after this start to the auction it's your bid:

| West | North | East | South |
|------|-------|------|-------|
|      |       | pass | pass  |
| 3◇   | dbl   | 5◇   | ?     |

Ignoring a dead ◊J, you have 9 HCP, only one loser in the opponents' suit and a decent five-card spade suit. It feels like they are sacrificing, but you are playing with a relatively new partner. Four choices present themselves:

1) Pass and see what partner does.
2) Double, which is clearly card-showing. Partner can bid or pass depending on her hand.
3) Bid 5♠ on the theory partner should have at least three for her double and may even have four.
4) Bid 5♡ on the theory partner should have at least three for her double and since you only have four, in all likelihood she has four herself. Better to play in a 4-4 fit than 5-3.

**Which do you go for?**

Frankly, I don't like any of the choices. Don't you hate it when people like East do things like bidding 5◊? He certainly learned to compete and make his opponents' lives difficult.

With choice 1), I worry we might be missing a cold slam somewhere. Partner must have a good hand to make a takeout double at the three-level. The problem with passing is that your partner doesn't learn much about your hand. She will have to assume you have a bust and that East's bid is based on strength. If partner doubles after your second pass, is it for penalty or again asking you to bid? Or is she letting you decide whether to leave the double in or bid? That depends on your partnership agreement, but pity poor partner if you force her to make the decision all on her own. Passing this hand asks too much of your partner. You have 9 potentially useful HCP, and partner needs to know about them.

The second choice, doubling, tells partner you have useful points, but doesn't tell much about the shape of your hand, other than that you don't have a standout long suit. Even if partner has a big club holding and pulls the double, your hand can help her make 6♣ — although you would much prefer she bid a major.

I stuck in choice 4) to be a bit facetious. Partner never seems to have the perfect hand to go with my misbids. And if you are making bids that only work if partner has a golden fit, I assure you those bids will come back to haunt you more often than not. With five spades and four hearts, the person I was playing with chose door number 3) and bid 5♠. Her thinking was that we should have enough points for game and with luck a 5-4 fit and enough power to take eleven tricks.

West passed. I had

♠A 10 9 8 ♡A 5 ◇A ♣A K 8 7 5 4

and I raised her to 6♠. (Given partner's free bid of 5♠, maybe I should have bid 7♠. But I didn't.)

Now let's see how this puppy plays. West leads the ♣2, and you ask me to display the whale you hope I have.

♠ A 10 9 8
♡ A 5
◇ A
♣ A K 8 7 5 4

♠ K J 5 3 2
♡ Q 10 4 3
◇ J
♣ Q J 6

**Plan your play and read on after you decide how to bring the contract home.**

Piece-o-cake, right? No club or diamond losers. Three possible heart losers, but once trumps are drawn, you can pitch the hearts on three good clubs. If you make sure to lose no more than one spade trick, the contract is golden. You give me your best smile, say 'Thank you, partner,' and call for a low club, which is ruffed by East with the ♠4. Your expletive does not pass your lips, but everyone at the table knows you thought it.

East returns the ♡2. **Plan your play again before reading on.**

Your original plan called for you to win all the tricks with the possible exception of a spade. You have lost the spade with that club ruff; if you bring in the remaining spades without another loss, the contract is still yours despite West's brilliant (or lucky) lead.

For a moment you wonder if the opponents are going to take the first four tricks with a crossruff. If they do, they do; nothing you can do about that. No reason not to play the ♡Q. West drops the ♡J. There are only three trumps outstanding. If they split 2-1 your ♠AK will clean them out and you can revert to Plan A and claim. If they are 3-0 you need to finesse against the queen and you can do it in either direction.

**Do you cash dummy's ♠A or your ♠K?**

Another way of asking this question is, 'Who is more likely to have the three remaining spades, East or West?' Recall the bidding for clues. You have the count on clubs (West has four) and West already played a heart. The only way West can have three spades is to have only five diamonds. Possible in some universes, but overwhelmingly unlikely in this one given the preemptive 3◊ bid. It's much more likely for West to have a spade void and East to have all the spades. If you have to finesse, it should be against East.

First lead up to dummy's ♠A: West reveals his void in spades. (Weren't you clever to figure that out?) Lead the ♠10 from dummy and when East eventually coughs up the ♠Q, finish drawing trumps. Now cash the two clubs in your hand, cross to dummy with your diamond, cash the rest of the clubs (discarding your hearts) and the slam is yours.

Unfortunately, what actually happened was this. My partner did not stop and replan as soon as the opponent played an unexpected card. She cashed the ♠K from her hand, discovered West's void and a second expletive failed to pass her lips. With no way to pick up the ♠Q, she was down one.

Here's the full deal:

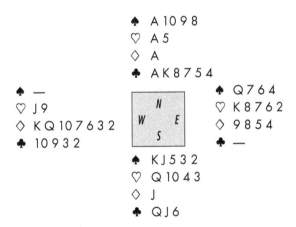

The real heroes on this deal were East-West. Their preemptive bidding caused my partner and me a lot of difficulty. We did end up in a good contract, but it was as much luck as skill. Partner could have bid 5♠ with a much poorer hand and then my leap to slam would not have worked well. Perhaps the stress of the auction contributed to my partner neglecting to recall that *plan first, then play* is important both at Trick 1 and after any trick that is a surprise or provides important new information.

And kudos to West for an inspired lead. Given his void in spades and his partner's support in diamonds, he probably figured either North or South had a diamond void, so he had no defensive tricks. If two hands had voids, why not a third — maybe partner! Given the number of hearts and clubs West had, it was more likely his partner would be void in clubs. Well, that's what I like to think, but maybe he just threw down the card farthest to the right in his hand. I'll never know because I didn't ask.

## PROBLEM 8

In fourth seat in a team game, neither side vulnerable, you sort your hand.

♠ A 3   ♡ 8   ◇ 10 6 5 4 3 2   ♣ 9 6 5 2

Your stomach growls near the end of a long match, and you wonder where to have lunch. South has been getting the cards all match and this deal is no exception. The bidding goes:

| West | North | East | South |
|------|-------|------|-------|
|      |       |      | 1♠ |
| 2♠[1] | 3♠ | pass | 4♠ |
| all pass |  |  |  |

1. Michaels, showing a two-suited hand with hearts and an unknown minor.

Partner leads the ◇7 and North displays dummy.

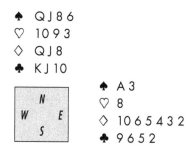

♠  Q J 8 6
♡  10 9 3
◇  Q J 8
♣  K J 10

♠  A 3
♡  8
◇  10 6 5 4 3 2
♣  9 6 5 2

Partner's 2♠ bid should promise five or more hearts and five or more of a minor. Assuming partner didn't cheat, the minor has to be clubs because there are only four diamonds missing. Partner is either leading a singleton or she has something like ◇K107, in which case she has no spades and declarer must have seven of them.

Declarer calls for the ◇Q from dummy, you play the ◇6. Since you can't cover, your attitude is obvious. Instead, you want to give partner the count, so you play your second highest card. Declarer follows with the ◇9 and immediately plays a low spade. You decide to win this trick with the ace: partner plays the ♠2, and declarer the ♠4.

**You're on lead now, so what shall it be?**

When in doubt, trust partner. She showed up with a spade, which means she can't have three diamonds to go along with her five hearts and spades. She probably would not lead a singleton diamond if she had no hope of getting a ruff. Therefore returning a diamond seems right. **Which diamond?**

Your only hope of another trick is if partner has the ♡A and gives you a heart ruff. Even if partner has six hearts, declarer has two of them so you will score your remaining trump. When you give partner a ruff, the card you play shows suit preference. Play the ◊10 to tell partner to lead hearts; she'll figure out the rest.

Declarer covers your ◊10 with the ◊A, partner ruffs and dummy plays low. Partner got the message and plays the ♡A, which holds, and then she leads the ♡2. You ruff with your remaining spade. **Now what do you play?**

Partner chose the ♡2 for a reason. Her card is suit preference for clubs. When you lead a club, partner cashes the ♣A and declarer claims the rest.

Down two. If you had listened to your stomach and continued to daydream your way toward lunch, you might have made the knee-jerk plays of either ducking the first spade trick or winning that trick and leading a heart to partner. Ducking the spade immediately gives them the contract. If you go up with the ♠A, but then lead a heart, how is partner to know you want a heart return? Your ♡8 isn't easy to read as a singleton. She might lead one out of desperation, but you should never count on luck when you have good plays at your disposal.

Here's the full deal:

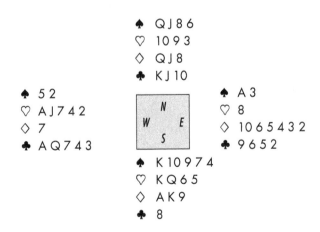

```
              ♠ Q J 8 6
              ♡ 10 9 3
              ◊ Q J 8
              ♣ K J 10
♠ 5 2                        ♠ A 3
♡ A J 7 4 2      N           ♡ 8
◊ 7          W       E       ◊ 10 6 5 4 3 2
♣ A Q 7 4 3      S           ♣ 9 6 5 2
              ♠ K 10 9 7 4
              ♡ K Q 6 5
              ◊ A K 9
              ♣ 8
```

# PROBLEM 9

In a team game sitting East, you heard the bidding go:

| West | North | East | South |
|------|-------|------|-------|
|      |       | pass | 1♠ |
| 3♡ | 3♠ | pass | 4♠ |
| all pass | | | |

Partner leads the ♡A and you watch carefully as dummy is displayed.

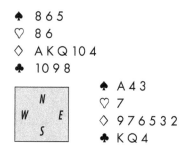

```
        ♠ 8 6 5
        ♡ 8 6
        ◇ A K Q 10 4
        ♣ 10 9 8
                    ♠ A 4 3
              N     ♡ 7
           W     E  ◇ 9 7 6 5 3 2
              S     ♣ K Q 4
```

North-South are vulnerable and you are not, so under your system, partner's third seat 3♡ bid promises a seven-bagger heart suit, but not much else beyond the ♡AK her lead suggests.

Declarer has already called for a small heart from dummy, which means he either has a clear line of play, or doesn't plan his play. You have no choice for the first trick, but you haven't completed figuring out your defense, so make them wait until you do. (Since you are following suit with a singleton, it is good ethics to say to declarer something like 'I have no problem on this trick' before you start thinking. You know exactly what card you are going to play to Trick 1, and you should not mislead declarer about that, intentionally or otherwise.)

Based on the bidding, you figure South probably has five or six spades to the ♠KQJ, three hearts, probably to the queen, no more than two diamonds and at least two clubs to the ace to justify his opening bid. Partner may have a spare jack floating around.

Partner can score two heart tricks, you can score the ♠A and your ♣KQ should be good for a trick. The fly in the ointment arrives if declarer can pitch his club losers in hand on dummy's four winning diamonds. Then your club trick disappears.

You play your heart and declarer tosses out the ♡10. Partner continues with the ♡K, dummy plays his heart and it's up to you. You desperately need partner to shift immediately to clubs so you can knock out declarer's ♣A. That way, when you get in with the ♠A you can score your winning club before declarer has pitched his club losers on dummy's diamonds.

Of course, once you've driven out declarer's ♣A, he may try to run his diamonds immediately to pitch the clubs, and you know that will work — unless partner has a spade (any spade, even the deuce will do). If partner has a spade, then declarer has only five, which means he must have at least five cards in the minors. At most he can get rid of three of them before partner ruffs — and you still have the ♠A for the setting trick.

*Visualizing necessity*, you put a spade in partner's hand. That done, you are back to your original problem: how can you guarantee that partner will not lead a third heart in the hopes you can overruff dummy. **Given the systems you use with your favorite partner, what card will you play?**

It's a trick question. No signaling method in the world will guarantee partner will do what must be done. You know the winning play, so don't allow partner to let you down. Take charge!

Ruff the second heart with a low trump (it doesn't cost anything) and lead the ♣K. Once you do that, declarer can wiggle and squirm, but won't come to more than nine tricks (and if he tries to dump losing clubs on good diamonds he will have to settle for eight tricks) because partner does indeed have the ♠2 to stop the possible parade of diamond winners. Here's the whole deal:

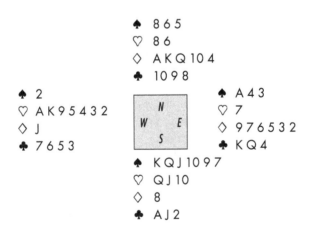

```
              ♠ 8 6 5
              ♡ 8 6
              ◇ A K Q 10 4
              ♣ 10 9 8
 ♠ 2                          ♠ A 4 3
 ♡ A K 9 5 4 3 2      N       ♡ 7
 ◇ J              W       E   ◇ 9 7 6 5 3 2
 ♣ 7 6 5 3           S        ♣ K Q 4
              ♠ K Q J 10 9 7
              ♡ Q J 10
              ◇ 8
              ♣ A J 2
```

Not only did you get to apply many of the Defense Disciplines (planning before playing, drawing inferences from the bidding and visualizing necessity) in this deal, your partner will be ever so happy that you took charge and defeated the contract.

## PROBLEM 10

Sitting West, here's your hand:

♠ A Q 5 2    ♡ 10 9 7 2    ♢ 8 6    ♣ K 4 3

I'll give you four different bidding sequences and you have to determine what you'll choose to lead.

(a) Neither side is vulnerable and scoring is IMPs.  **What's your lead?**

| West | North | East | South |
|------|-------|------|-------|
|      |       |      | 1◇ |
| pass | 3◇¹ | pass | 3♡² |
| pass | 3♠³ | pass | 4◇ |
| all pass |    |      |      |

1. Limit raise in diamonds.
2. Heart suit.
3. Requests partner to bid 3NT with a spade stopper.

Because you were not clear about the meanings of their bids, before you decided your lead you asked specifically about the 3◇, 3♡ and 3♠ bids and received the explanations shown above.  You conclude from the bidding that (1) they have a lot of diamonds, (2) South has a heart stopper, (3) North has a club stopper (because he was willing to play 3NT as long as partner had a spade stopper) and (4) because of the emphasis on bidding games in IMP scoring you can bank on neither one having spades stopped.

If either North or South held the ♠Kx(x) they would have bid 3NT.  Some pairs play that North should have at least a partial stopper in spades to make the 3♠ bid. When asked, this pair did not mention it.  Figure North has at best Jxx in spades.

Normally you would not want to lead away from an AQ tenace in a suit contract.  Here you 'know' partner has the ♣K, so go ahead and lead your ♠A.

(b) Here's a second auction.  You still hold

♠ A Q 5 2    ♡ 10 9 7 2    ♢ 8 6    ♣ K 4 3

With both sides vulnerable and playing MPs, **what do you plan to lead this time?**

| West | North | East | South |
|------|-------|------|-------|
|      |       |      | 1♠ |
| pass | 2◇¹ | pass | 2♡ |
| pass | 3◇ | pass | 3NT |
| all pass |    |      |      |

1. Game force.

What do we know from the bidding? South likely has five spades, four hearts and four cards in the minors. North has opening points and six diamonds. He does not have three spades or four hearts. They strongly bid to game, although they may not have the best fit in the world.

Listening to the bidding can suggest whether you should sit back and make declarer work to set up his tricks or fire a rocket, which can have spectacular (good or bad) results. The more strongly the opponents bid to game the more likely you need to find an attacking lead. With this bidding, if you wait around for your tricks, you are going to find diamonds crammed down your throat.

Notrump contracts are races. With dummy's diamonds hanging over your head, you need to come out charging at the opening bell (your lead). Spades would be suicide — let him try to set up something there. You and declarer have the same number of hearts and given your spots, his are probably better. We know who has the diamond suit. That leaves clubs. If North had a good club stopper he would probably have bid 3NT himself. There is no reason not to hope partner has an honor or two and a bit of length in clubs.

Well, hope is one thing, but is there a decent reason why partner could indeed have an honor or two in clubs? North-South have game points between them, but some may be coming from North's diamond length. You only have 9 HCP. Credit them with 23-27 HCP, which leaves partner with 4-8. If it's your lucky day, partner's points could include the ♣AJ10. I'd choose to lead the ♣3 and hope to trap the queen I suspect declarer might have.

(c) This time North-South blast to game. You still hold

♠A Q 5 2  ♡10 9 7 2  ◇8 6  ♣K 4 3

They are vulnerable, you are not in this matchpoint-scored game. **What do you plan to lead?**

| West | North | East | South |
|------|-------|------|-------|
|      |       |      | 1NT[1] |
| pass | 3NT | all pass | |

1. 15-17 HCP.

What do we know from the bidding? After South's strong notrump opener, North directly bid game. North must have at least 10 points and probably does not have a four-card major since he did not use Stayman. (He could also have a flattish hand and expect to take as many tricks in notrump as in a major and be after the extra 10 points notrump contracts earn.)

South could have a four- or even five-card major. (Their convention card indicates that they frequently open 1NT holding a five-card major.) Despite all those caveats, all other things being equal, it still makes sense to attack the majors.

You know South has 15-17 HCP. Figure North for at least 10 HCP in order to rocket to game — that's a minimum of 25 HCP. With your 9 HCP, partner has at most 6 HCP and probably fewer.

Even though their bidding calls for an attacking lead, your hand suggests it is better to sit back and force declarer to come to you. With your tenace in spades and only four of them, leading those is not attractive. (With five or, preferably, six spades you might consider it.) You have nothing in diamonds. Leading a diamond will only suck whatever honor partner might hold out of her hand without any advantage to your side. For a club lead to work, partner needs an honor, but you don't know that she has one.

Three suits down, hearts are left. If the opponents are short in hearts, you are making a good start at setting up length tricks. With your spade honors, you have a good chance of being able to lead hearts again if partner is favorably disposed to the suit. I'd try the ♡10.

(d) This time North-South stop in a partscore.

♠A Q 5 2   ♡10 9 7 2   ◇8 6   ♣K 4 3

You are vulnerable; they are not. **What do you plan to lead?**

| West | North | East | South |
|------|-------|------|-------|
|      |       |      | 1♠ |
| pass | 1NT | pass | 2◇ |
| all pass |       |      |    |

What have we learned from the bidding? Quite a lot, when you think about it. South has at least five spades and North has fewer than three since he didn't support them. They probably have a 4-4 diamond fit, although it could be a 4-3 fit if North had a singleton or void in spades. Partner had two chances to bid: once after North's 1NT and a second time in the passout seat to reopen the bidding. She didn't squeak either time so she either doesn't have enough points or a good enough suit to bid at the two-level. She isn't shapely with lots of clubs and hearts or she might have reopened with a double.

You're left with a lot of vague ideas that will become clearer as the play continues, but right now you concentrate on two facts: (1) North preferred diamonds to spades, and (2) you have winning spades in the ♠AQ sitting behind South. You want to make sure to score those tricks, and the only way you won't is if North's hand ruffs them away (or you are forced to lead spades).

Well, you're not going to lead spades now; that's for sure. Since you are concerned about possible ruffs in dummy, the best way to eliminate that threat is to lead trumps. Pick your favorite diamond and let 'er rip.

Notice with the same hand we ended up leading four different cards from four different suits — all based on the scoring method, our opponents' bidding and our partner's passes.

## PROBLEM 11

Both sides are vulnerable on this deal. After the bidding shown below, West leads the ♡10 and dummy is displayed. **Plan your play.**

| West | North | East | South |
|------|-------|------|-------|
|      |       |      | 1NT   |
| pass | 2♡¹   | pass | 2♠    |
| all pass |    |      |       |

1. Transfer.

> ♠ J 10 5 4 3
> ♡ J 3 2
> ◇ Q J 9
> ♣ 4 3
>
> ▭
>
> ♠ A 9 2
> ♡ K Q 5
> ◇ A K 10
> ♣ J 8 5 2

As is often the case when transfer bids are involved, it is easier to count losers using dummy reversal. I figured there were two possible losers in spades, one heart, no diamonds and two clubs. Should be a breeze, I thought at the end of a long day. (You'd think that by now I would be wary anytime I start thinking about breezes. Hurricanes start with breezes too.) In fact, if I can capture one of the missing spade honors with my ace, I can make an overtrick. The opponents are playing standard carding — nothing fancy.

East produces the ♡A and, to create a second entry in dummy, I dropped the ♡Q under it. East switched to the ◇8, which I allowed to ride around to dummy's ◇J in order to take a spade finesse. (West played the ◇2.) In order to retain the lead in dummy should the finesse succeed, I led the ♠J from dummy. (Because I have the ♠J109 between the two hands, leading an honor is fine.) East played the ♠7, I ducked and West won the trick with the ♠K. West thought for a bit and slid a low diamond onto the table. East played the ◇7 (completing a high-low), and I captured the trick in hand with the ◇A.

My original plan was to use the ♡J as an entry to dummy and, once there, take a second spade finesse to capture the ♠Q. Two questions for you: **Is this still the right course of action? Does your answer change if this is a team match (IMPs) rather than a pairs game (MPs)?**

When considering my plan after the opening lead, I figured I could lose five tricks and still make the contract. They consisted of two spade losers, one heart and two clubs. The heart is already lost and I have the two high hearts remaining. There is still nowhere to hide the two club losers. The contract depends on losing at most two spade tricks, one of which is already a goner. Thus, to make the contract, I must hold my spade losses to one. If I can win all the spade tricks, I'll get an overtrick.

We know a couple of other things that help us make our decision. East gave a high-low signal in diamonds (showing an even number of diamonds) with the ♢8 and ♢7, and West indicated an odd number of diamonds with the initial play of the ♢2. With seven diamonds between them, assuming no lies, East has two or four and West has five or three.

Three spades remain: the Q, 8 and 6. My original plan was to lead a low heart, win the trick in dummy and then lead a spade to finesse the ♠Q. Is there any combination of spades that will cause me to throw away the contract?

Yes, if West has the ♠Q and East the ♠86. West will win with the queen and lead a diamond, which East will ruff if he started with a doubleton.

In IMPs, there is no reason to take that risk. I can afford to lose one spade trick. Regardless of who holds which remaining spades, if I play the ♠A, I will lose at most one spade trick, guaranteeing the contract. In fact, if either opponent has the bare ♠Q, that play will score an overtrick.

However, you can score an overtrick twice as often by taking the finesse as by laying down the ace, and so at matchpoints the odds are mathematically in your favor for trying the finesse. A question you could ask is what other pairs will do. Some I/Ns won't create the second entry in dummy by dropping the ♡Q on the first trick. Those pairs can't take the second finesse even if they want to because they have no way to get to dummy. Their only choice is to play the ace and settle for making the contract. Remembering the adage in pairs games to 'score positive', some pairs may play the ace and be thankful they made the contract.

This deal came from a pairs game, and I took the finesse. Here's the whole deal:

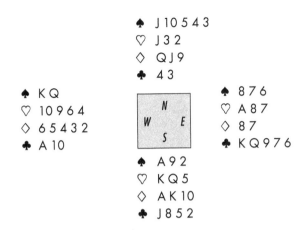

```
              ♠ J 10 5 4 3
              ♡ J 3 2
              ◇ Q J 9
              ♣ 4 3
♠ K Q                        ♠ 8 7 6
♡ 10 9 6 4        N          ♡ A 8 7
◇ 6 5 4 3 2   W       E      ◇ 8 7
♣ A 10            S          ♣ K Q 9 7 6
              ♠ A 9 2
              ♡ K Q 5
              ◇ A K 10
              ♣ J 8 5 2
```

Analyzing the play **double dummy**, East-West can hold the contract to +110 by cashing two clubs, ending with East, who leads the third club for West to ruff. West reenters East's hand with the ♡A and gets a second ruff on another club lead. If you watched East-West reel off the first five tricks, you might feel picked on. No matter. Congratulate your opponents on fine defense and pick up the next hand.

I would have been much better off if East-West had found the perfect defense! When I took the finesse, West scored the ♣Q, played back a diamond that East ruffed, and I was down one for -100 and a near bottom. My big mistake was not realizing most of the field would not take the second finesse.

Hey, I didn't say I won them all.


## PROBLEM 12

Sometimes bidding is not a problem. In a team game, you pick up

♠A 6 4 ♡A K 9 ◇Q 10 ♣A K 6 5 2

With 20 HCP and 3-3-2-5 distribution you choose a 2NT opening, figuring the five-card club suit makes up for the doubleton diamond. Partner jumps to 6NT and after three passes West leads the ♣Q. Partner displays dummy and it's time for your plan before you read any further.

```
        ♠ K 7 5
        ♡ J 10 4
        ◇ A K J 7 2
        ♣ J 8

        ♠ A 6 4
        ♡ A K 9
        ◇ Q 10
        ♣ A K 6 5 2
```

It's notrump, so you start by counting winners. You have eleven off the top: two spades, two hearts, five diamonds and two clubs. Checking the suits for developmental tricks you find none in spades. Hearts looks attractive with a 50/50 shot of the ♡Q being onside. Nothing further to be gained in diamonds. You have a seven-card club fit, so if they split 3-3 (36%) you can lose one club and score another.

So far hearts looks best, but you also have a 50-50 finesse in clubs: you can lead low from hand toward the ♣J. If West has the ♣Q and ducks, you immediately get your twelfth trick. If East has the ♣Q, you can still score an extra club trick if clubs split 3-3.

So clubs gives you two chances and hearts only one. Is there any other reason to test clubs before trying hearts? You betcha; glad you asked. If you try the heart finesse and it fails, you can no longer lead up to the ♣J because whoever has the ♣Q will take the trick for down one. Even if everything fails in clubs, then as long as you have an entry to dummy you can still try the 50-50 heart finesse.

Which brings us to the topic of dummy entries. How many do you have for certain? Just the ♠K. If diamonds are so rude as to split 5-1 or 6-0, you can't afford to overtake the ◇Q or ◇10 in dummy. Yes, those splits rarely happen, but this is a bridge book, so they are somewhat more likely. (Just kidding. But if you can avoid a problem with even unlikely splits there is no reason to do anything ill-advised like take your ♠K on the first trick and leave only diamonds as sure entries.)

If you are lucky, West holds the ♣Q and dummy's ♣J will provide a second entry. Let's not count on luck — you duck the first spade into your hand and win the ♠A.

Trick 2: Being prudent on Trick 1 allows you to find out if it really is your lucky day and someone has the singleton ♡Q. The odds are miniscule, but if Her Majesty drops, all your worries are over and it costs nothing to try. Play the ♡A. No ♡Q appears.

Trick 3: Before the opponents understand more about your hand, lead a low club toward the ♣J. West plays low. East wins your jack with his queen. Alternative #1 has been unsuccessfully eliminated.

Trick 4: East proceeds to knock out your spade entry by leading a small spade.

Trick 5: Time to try the second part of the club scenario and find out if they split 3-3, in which case you are again home free. Why not try the heart finesse with the last sure entry in dummy? While the clubs breaking 3-3 is odds against, the chances of diamonds breaking 5-1 or worse are much, much smaller. You should take the risk of not scoring all five diamonds because you have to overtake one of declarer's diamonds in order to take the heart finesse. So lead a small club to your ♣A. Everyone follows. So far, so good.

Trick 6: Play your ♣K in hopes of gathering in two more clubs and promoting your remaining clubs to winners. No go. East discards a spade. You can pitch the worthless spade (you still have one in hand in case West, who obviously started with ♣QJ10x, accidently throws them all away while you run diamonds). West has the boss club now. You are going to have to try the heart finesse to bring home the contract. To do that, you need to use diamonds to enter dummy.

Trick 7: Play the ◇Q. Everyone follows.

Trick 8: Play the ◇10 and overtake in dummy. Everyone follows. Yippee, your diamonds run.

Trick 9: Start to run diamonds. East follows suit. You can afford to pitch a club and West pitches a heart.

Trick 10: Lead your next diamond. You and West both pitch spades.

Trick 11: Lead your final diamond. East discards a heart, you and West both pitch your last clubs.

Trick 12: It's all come down to this trick. If East has the ♡Q you make your slam. Call for the ♡J. East plays a low heart, and your jack wins the trick. Success!

Here's the whole deal:

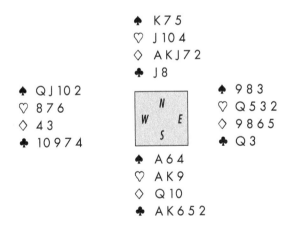

```
              ♠ K 7 5
              ♡ J 10 4
              ◇ A K J 7 2
              ♣ J 8
♠ Q J 10 2          N          ♠ 9 8 3
♡ 8 7 6                        ♡ Q 5 3 2
◇ 4 3          W       E       ◇ 9 8 6 5
♣ 10 9 7 4          S          ♣ Q 3
              ♠ A 6 4
              ♡ A K 9
              ◇ Q 10
              ♣ A K 6 5 2
```

All that work and if you had just done what most finesseaholics would do before reading this book (just take that heart finesse right away) you would have scored twelve tricks 'the easy way'. All that thinking and planning. Why waste the energy?

Because on the next deal, West will have both the ♣Q and the ♡Q and you'll make the contract and they won't.

## PROBLEM 13 (THE FINAL EXAM)

Here's your last board of the day. You've been having a good session, but a niggling whisper in your head hints that playing this one right is for all the marbles. On this deal everyone is vulnerable. You sort your hand and find an opener with 16 HCP and 4-2-5-2 distribution:

♠ A Q 8 3    ♡ A K    ◇ K 10 8 6 2    ♣ 8 4

However you choose to open this — I'd try 1NT, but others might object to the two doubletons and plan to start with 1◇ — partner drives you to a 3NT contract.

Through the magic of bridge book technology you get to play this using both IMP and MP scoring. While you settle in with that idea, West leads the ♠J and North says, 'Good luck, partner. It either works or it doesn't.'

Plan your play, first scoring in IMPs.

```
            ♠  7 6 5
            ♡  9 4 2
            ◇  7
            ♣  A K Q 6 3 2
            ┌──────────┐
            └──────────┘
            ♠  A Q 8 3
            ♡  A K
            ◇  K 10 8 6 2
            ♣  8 4
```

It's notrump, so you start by counting winners. You have seven off the top since West was kind enough to lead into your spade tenace. Clubs will provide three extra tricks if you get the normal 3-2 break in the suit, which you know has a good chance (68%). You have exactly zero entries to the clubs other than the clubs themselves. The only other place to collect a trick is in diamonds if East has the ace or if West leads them. Expecting West to lead diamonds after he sees dummy is asking a lot, especially since he was so nice to give you the spade trick on the lead.

Ten tricks are nice only if we can make sure of nine. If clubs break 5-0, you can't score nine tricks, so ignore that possibility. However, if clubs break 4-1 the simple safety play of ducking a club in both hands guarantees the game — as long as you can withstand any lead East-West can make. You have the top card in all suits except diamonds, where a lead by West sets up your king. West is no problem; how about East?

Can you survive a diamond lead from East? Yes, the ◇K10xx will see you through. If East wins the safety club trick and leads a low diamond, play the ◇10. West wins, but finds himself in the same position as before. If East leads either the ◇Q or ◇J, cover with the ◇K. West presumably wins with the ◇A, but with him on lead, your ◇10 is a stopper.

At IMPs the play is clear. At Trick 2 lead a low club toward dummy and, regardless of what West plays, play low. If clubs are the expected 3-2 you have given them an extra trick and 1 IMP. If clubs break 4-1, you've just saved yourself 12 IMPs. With no doubts about your decision, at IMPs go for the safety play and guarantee your contract.

Having solved the IMPs problem, you are immediately teleported to a MP pairs game and discover you are in the same 3NT contract. West has again led the ♠J and you are faced with the same decision about how to tackle clubs. With the safety play, nine tricks are in the bag, but the extra trick could mean the difference between a great session and one not quite so great. It's that close. Do you feel the pressure?

Remember, at matchpoints it's all about frequency. You expect the 3-2 club split 68% of the time and the 4-1 on only 28% of deals. (See Appendix B, page 162, if you don't remember these odds.) The other 4% is the 5-0 split that would cause everyone to go down. Before you decide, let me give you one more piece of information: on the first trick, East put up the ♠K. That spade finesse always works, even if West doesn't give it to you on the opening lead.

No-longer-Timid Timothy of preemptive fame whispers in your ear that this too is a no-brainer. You have to go with the odds, which are 70% in your favor to score the extra trick. Cash your clubs.

The whole deal? Hey, are you an optimist or a pessimist? If I had to show the whole deal, I'd need the publisher to print 30% of the books with a deal in which you go down and 70% of the books with a layout where you score the extra trick. He said no. That's life in the bridge world.

Know that you made the right decision, no matter the actual result. Pick up your next hand and start on a new adventure.


## A LAST WORD

You've reached the end. Now it's up to you. Don't try to incorporate all of the thirty-five major tips at once. Select a few to work on first, and when you are comfortable with those, then move on to some others. Most of all, have fun. I hope to see you at the bridge table!

# Appendix A:

# ACBL CONVENTION CARD

## SPECIAL DOUBLES

After Overcall: Penalty☐ _____
Negative☐  thru_____
Responsive☐ : thru _____Maximal☐
Support: Dbl.☐ thru _____Redbl☐
Card-showing☐  Min. Offshape T/O☐

## SIMPLE OVERCALL

1 level_____to_____HCP (usually)
often 4 cards☐  very light style☐

### Responses

New Suit: Forcing☐ NFConst☐ NF☐
Jump Raise: Forcing☐ Inv.☐ Weak☐

## JUMP OVERCALL

Strong☐   Intermediate☐   Weak☐
_____

## OPENING PREEMPTS

|  | Sound | Light | Very Light |
|---|---|---|---|
| 3/4-bids | ☐ | ☐ | ☐ |

Conv./Resp. _____

## DIRECT CUEBID

|  | OVER: Minor | Major |
|---|---|---|
| Natural | ☐ | ☐ |
| Strong T/O | ☐ | ☐ |
| Michaels | ☐ | ☐ |

## NOTRUMP OVERCALLS

Direct: _____to_____Systems on☐
Conv.☐ _____
Balancing: _____to_____
Jump to 2NT: Minors☐  2 Lowest☐
Conv.☐ _____

## DEFENSE VS NOTRUMP

| vs: | | |
|---|---|---|
| 2♣ | _____ | _____ |
| 2♦ | _____ | _____ |
| 2♥ | _____ | _____ |
| 2♠ | _____ | _____ |
| Dbl: | _____ | _____ |
| Other | _____ | _____ |

## OVER OPP'S T/O DOUBLE

New Suit Forcing: 1 level☐ 2 level☐
Jump Shift: Forcing☐ Inv.☐ Weak☐
Redouble implies no fit☐

| 2NT Over | Limit+ | Limit | Weak |
|---|---|---|---|
| Majors | ☐ | ☐ | ☐ |
| Minors | ☐ | ☐ | ☐ |

Other_____

## VS Opening Preempts Double Is

Takeout☐ thru _____ Penalty☐
Conv. Takeout: _____
Lebensohl 2NT Response☐
Other: _____

## SLAM CONVENTIONS

Gerber☐ :   4NT: Blackwood☐  RKC☐  1430☐

vs Interference: DOPI☐  DEPO☐  Level: _____ ROPI☐

## LEADS (circle card led, if not in bold)

| versus Suits | | versus Notrump | |
|---|---|---|---|
| **X X** | x x x **x** | **X X** | x x x **x** |
| x x **X** | x x x **X** x | **X** x x | x x x **X** x |
| A K x | **T** 9 x | A **K** J x | A **Q** J x |
| **K** Q x | K **J** T x | A **J** T 9 | A **T** 9 x |
| **Q** J x | K **T** 9 x | **K** Q J x | K **Q** T 9 |
| **J** T 9 | Q **T** 9 x | **Q** J T x | Q **T** 9 x |
| **K** Q T 9 | | **J** T 9 x | **T** 9 x x |

### LENGTH LEADS:

4th Best            vs SUITS☐  vs NT☐
3rd/5th Best     vs SUITS☐  vs NT☐
                        Attitude vs NT☐

### Primary signal to partner's leads

Attitude☐   Count☐   Suit preference☐

## DEFENSIVE CARDING

| | vs SUITS | vs NT |
|---|---|---|
| Standard: | ☐ | ☐ |
| Except ☐ | | |

| Upside-Down: | | |
|---|---|---|
| count | ☐ | ☐ |
| attitude | ☐ | ☐ |

### FIRST DISCARD

| | | |
|---|---|---|
| Lavinthal | ☐ | ☐ |
| Odd/Even | ☐ | ☐ |
| | ☐ | ☐ |

### OTHER CARDING

| | | |
|---|---|---|
| Smith Echo | ☐ | ☐ |
| Trump Suit Pref. | ☐ | |
| Foster Echo | ☐ | ☐ |

## SPECIAL CARDING ☐   PLEASE ASK

NAMES _____

## GENERAL APPROACH

**Two Over One:** Game Forcing ☐  Game Forcing Except When Suit Rebid ☐
**VERY LIGHT:** Openings ☐  3rd Hand ☐  Overcalls ☐  Preempts ☐
**FORCING OPENING:** 1♣ ☐  2♣ ☐  Natural 2 Bids ☐  Other ☐ _____

### NOTRUMP OPENING BIDS

| | | |
|---|---|---|
| 1NT | | |
| ____ to ____ | 3♣ _____ | |
| ____ to ____ | 3♦ _____ | |
| 5-card Major common ☐ | 3♥ _____ | |
| System on over ____ | 3♠ _____ | |
| 2♣ Stayman ☐ Puppet ☐ | _____ | |
| 2♦ Transfer to ♥ ☐ | 4♦ , 4♥ Transfer ☐ | |
| Forcing Stayman ☐ | Smolen ☐ | |
| 2♥ Transfer to ♠ ☐ | Lebensohl ☐ (____denies) | |
| 2♠ _____ | Neg. Double ☐: _____ | |
| 2NT _____ | Other: _____ | |

**2NT** ____ to ____
Puppet Stayman ☐
**Transfer Responses:**
Jacoby ☐   Texas ☐
3♠ _____

**3NT** ____ to ____

**Conventional NT Openings**
_____

### MAJOR OPENING

| | | 4 | 5 |
|---|---|---|---|
| Expected Min. Length | | | |
| 1st/2nd | | ☐ | ☐ |
| 3rd/4th | | ☐ | ☐ |

#### RESPONSES
Double Raise: Force ☐  Inv. ☐  Weak ☐
After Overcall: Force ☐  Inv. ☐  Weak ☐
Conv. Raise: 2NT ☐  3NT ☐  Splinter ☐
Other: _____
1NT: Forcing ☐  Semi-forcing ☐
2NT: Forcing ☐  Inv. ☐ ____ to ____
3NT: ____ to ____
Drury ☐ : Reverse ☐  2-Way ☐  Fit ☐
Other: _____

### MINOR OPENING

| | | 4 | 3 | NF 0–2 | Conv. |
|---|---|---|---|---|---|
| Expected Min. Length | | | | | |
| 1♣ | | ☐ | ☐ | ☐ | ☐ |
| 1♦ | | ☐ | ☐ | ☐ | ☐ |

#### RESPONSES
Double Raise: Force ☐  Inv. ☐  Weak ☐
After Overcall: Force ☐  Inv. ☐  Weak ☐
Forcing Raise: J/S in other minor ☐
Single raise ☐  Other: _____
Frequently bypass 4+ ♦ ☐
1NT/1♣ _____ to _____
2NT Forcing ☐  Inv. ☐ ____ to ____
3NT: ____ to ____
Other _____

### DESCRIBE    RESPONSES/REBIDS

| | |
|---|---|
| **2♣** ____ to ____ HCP | |
| Strong ☐  Other ☐ | _____ |
| 2♦ Resp: Neg ☐  Waiting ☐ | |
| **2♦** ____ to ____ HCP | |
| Natural: Weak ☐ Intermediate ☐ Strong ☐  Conv. ☐ | 2NT Force ☐ New Suit NF ☐ |
| **2♥** ____ to ____ HCP | |
| Natural: Weak ☐ Intermediate ☐ Strong ☐  Conv. ☐ | 2NT Force ☐ New Suit NF ☐ |
| **2♠** ____ to ____ HCP | |
| Natural: Weak ☐ Intermediate ☐ Strong ☐  Conv. ☐ | 2NT Force ☐ New Suit NF ☐ |

**OTHER CONV. CALLS:** New Minor Forcing: ☐  2-Way NMF ☐
Weak Jump Shifts: In Comp. ☐  Not in Comp. ☐ _____
4th Suit Forcing: 1 Rd. ☐  Game ☐ _____
_____
_____

# Appendix B:

# SUIT SPLIT PROBABILITIES

Throughout this book we have referenced suit split probabilities. Below is a chart that shows the probabilities of the different splits. You can memorize them if you wish. It's not too painful and will provide useful guidance as you are playing hands at the table. If you prefer to just have a "good feel" for how a suit might split, you can use the shading to give you a sense of how likely a split is. The lighter the background, the more likely the split. The darker the background, the more unlikely that particular split will occur. (But when they do occur, dark results are more likely.)

To use this chart, first determine how many cards are outstanding in the suit. For example, if you are playing in an eight-card heart fit, there are five cards outstanding. The chances are good (68%) that the suit splits 3-2. Here are three handy points you can glean from the chart without memorizing any details.

1) If you have an odd number of cards outstanding, the chances of them splitting as close to even as possible are good or very good.
2) With an even number of cards outstanding, there is an about average chance that the suit splits one off from even. For example with six cards outstanding, you can expect a 4-2 split about 48% of the time.
3) With an even number of cards outstanding (greater than two) the chances of an even split are always less than average.

| Cards Outstanding in Suit | Split | Likelihood | Percentage* |
|---|---|---|---|
| 2 | 1-1 | AVERAGE | 52% |
| 2 | 2-0 | AVERAGE | 48% |
| 3 | 2-1 | VERY GOOD | 78% |
| 3 | 3-0 | POOR | 22% |
| 4 | 2-2 | FAIR | 40% |
| 4 | 3-1 | AVERAGE | 50% |
| 4 | 4-0 | POOR | 10% |
| 5 | 3-2 | GOOD | 68% |
| 5 | 4-1 | POOR | 28% |
| 5 | 5-0 | BAD | 4% |

| Cards Outstanding in Suit | Split | Likelihood | Percentage* |
|---|---|---|---|
| 6 | 3-3 | FAIR | 36% |
| 6 | 4-2 | AVERAGE | 48% |
| 6 | 5-1 | POOR | 15% |
| 6 | 6-0 | BAD | 1% |
| 7 | 4-3 | GOOD | 62% |
| 7 | 5-2 | POOR | 31% |
| 7 | 6-1 | BAD | 7% |
| 7 | 7-0 | BAD | 1% |
| 8 | 4-4 | POOR | 33% |
| 8 | 5-3 | AVERAGE | 47% |
| 8 | 6-2 | BAD | 17% |
| 8 | 7-1 | BAD | 3% |
| 8 | 8-0 | BAD | 0% |

\* Percentages may not add to 100% because of rounding.

# GLOSSARY

**2/1 system**
A popular modern variant of standard bidding in which an initial two-level response in a new suit over an opening suit bid is forcing to game.

**ACBL**
American Contract Bridge League — the body which runs tournaments in North America and issues masterpoints.

**Alert**
Often, when partner makes a conventional bid, you must alert the opponents, which allows them to ask its meaning if they wish. The ACBL convention card shows alertable bids in red.

**Average-minus**
A below average score on a deal.

**Average-plus**
An above average score on a deal.

**Convention Card**
A sheet of paper showing your partnership agreements regarding bidding, leads and defensive carding. You must make your convention card available to your opponents. See Appendix A (page 160) for a sample convention card.

**Double Dummy**
Refers to playing the cards already knowing what is in all four hands.

**Dummy Points**
Total points in your hand including HCP and distributional points based on the assumption your partner will become declarer and your hand will be dummy in support of partner's suit (sometimes also referred to as support points).

**Dummy Reversal**
A technique in playing the hand that treats the dummy as the 'main hand' and declarer as the subsidiary hand. It is most useful for counting losers and planning the play when dummy has an equal or longer trump suit.

**Falsecard**
Playing a misleading card in order to deceive an opponent.

| | |
|---|---|
| **Favorable Vulnerability** | Your side is not vulnerable and the loyal opposition is vulnerable. |
| **HCP** | High-card points. The most common count is: ace = 4; king = 3; queen = 2; jack = 1. |
| **IMPs** | International Matchpoints — a mechanism for converting differences in raw scores to a scale to compare results from competing teams or pairs. |
| **I/N** | Intermediate/Novice — denotes a level of playing skill (often self-described) or at tournaments may indicate a separate playing section for those with fewer than a specified number of masterpoints. |
| **Jacoby 2NT** | A conventional 2NT response to a major-suit opening, made with four-card or better support of the major and a game forcing hand. |
| **LHO** | Left-Hand Opponent. |
| **Life Master** | Once the highest rank in most bridge-playing countries. The ACBL now has six ranks of Life Master. |
| **Masterpoints** | Awarded by clubs and at tournaments to reflect placement in events. Masterpoints measure cumulative achievement in competition and do not necessarily indicate skill level (although if you lose to someone with 20,000+ masterpoints, you should suspect it wasn't just luck). |
| **Matchpoints (MPs)** | A mechanism for comparing your pair's result to all others who played the same deal. You receive one matchpoint for each pair sitting in the same direction as you whose score you beat and one-half matchpoint for each score tied with your pair. |
| **Red X** | The 'double' card in a bidding box, which is red with a big X on it. Redouble is a staid blue with XX. |
| **RHO** | Right-Hand Opponent. |

| | |
|---|---|
| **Rule of Eleven** | When the fourth-best card from a suit is led, subtracting the spotcard value from eleven gives the number of higher cards in the suit among the other three hands. |
| **Strain** | One of the four suits or notrump. |
| **Support Points** | see **Dummy Points** |
| **Tenace** | A combination of two cards (usually high or relatively high) of the same suit in one hand with one card ranking two degrees below the other. For example: ♡AQ or ♣KJ. |
| **Trump echo** | A high-low signal in the trump suit, indicating extra trump length and an ability to ruff. |

# SUGGESTED READING LIST

I have learned *something* from every bridge book I've read, even those I would only recommend as doorstops. Certain books I have found particularly useful in helping me understand and improve different aspects of my bridge game.

Bergen, Marty
> *More Points Schmoints!* My early mentor, John Baity, suggested this book to me as a tutorial on better incorporating shape in my bidding decisions. He was right.
> *Slam Bidding Made Easier* takes the same approach of reflecting shape in bidding with big hands.

Boehm, Augie
> *Matchpoints vs. IMPs.* Once I got serious about understanding the differences in these two forms of scoring, I found Boehm's book very helpful.

Bourke, Tim & Marc Smith
> *Countdown to Winning Bridge* is not for the neophyte bridge player. Bridge experts counsel that counting the hand is key to stronger bridge. When you decide to make a commitment toward counting, this book has a lot of practical ideas and useful tips for learning how to do it. I read the book, but there is also software covering the same material.

Cohen, Larry
> *To Bid or Not to Bid* was the best-selling bridge book of its time (the early 1990s), and its clear presentation of the Law of Total Tricks went a long way in helping me make better bidding decisions.

Dufresne, Mary Ann & Marion Ellingsen
> *Bridge with Bells & Whistles* provides lots of good material when you realize your basic bidding system doesn't quite get the job done. If at the end of a round you're frequently asking, 'How should we have bid that?' then chances are you can find the answer here.

Kantar, Eddie
> I haven't yet found an Eddie (or Edwin B. in his more formal persona) Kantar book I haven't enjoyed. The two listed below were the most helpful early in my bridge education. I used the software, but they are also available in book format.
> *Eddie Kantar Teaches Modern Bridge Defense*
> *Eddie Kantar Teaches Advanced Bridge Defense*

As I became a stronger player (which is significantly different from being a strong player) I found many useful tips in *Take Your Tricks*. It's a book I read again and again.

Lawrence, Mike

*How to Read Your Opponents' Cards*. As I read this book I had a number of 'aha' moments.

*The Complete Book of Overcalls in Contract Bridge* (2nd Edition). Once you get past the basics of overcalling, it's time to starting reading this book. Some sections are more advanced, but you can always leave them for later.

Rodwell, Eric & Mark Horton

*The Rodwell Files* is intended primarily for advanced players. However, as I sample various topics, I am convinced those of us with less than advanced experience can also pick up many useful nuggets from Rodwell and Horton's work. Those currently at the intermediate skill level should consider this a book to read and ponder in small doses rather than one to read straight through.

Root, William S.

Two classics that continue to prove useful, even if they are occasionally a little dated, are *How to Defend a Bridge Hand* and *How to Play a Bridge Hand*.

Roth, Danny

*Focus on Declarer Play*. When I finished reading this book I had a much better understanding of how and why I was leaving tricks on the table as a declarer.

Seagram, Barbara & Marc Smith

*25 Bridge Conventions You Should Know* is a handy resource when you decide to methodically add conventions to your knowledge base. It's the best-selling bridge book of the last fifty years for a good reason.

Thurston, Paul

*Bridge: 25 Steps to Learning 2/1*. This is the book I picked up when I decided I had to learn what the 2/1 bidding system was all about. Even if you want to continue to play 'Standard American,' this book will let you in on what your opponents' bids mean.

Watson, Louis D.

*Play of the Hand* is the classic bible of bridge play (at least prior to the publication of *The Rodwell Files*). Some of the material is basic, some perhaps too advanced and much of it perfect for intermediate players. As your skill improves, each read through brings additional understanding.